Poets in Person

at The Glassblower

First Edition: Poets in Person
First published in Great Britain in 2014 by:
Indigo Dreams Publishing Ltd
24 Forest Houses
Cookworthy Moor
Halwill
Beaworthy
EX21 5UU
UK
www.indigodreams.co.uk

ISBN 978-1-909357-41-9

British Library Cataloguing in Publication Data. A CIP record for this book can be obtained from the British Library.

Designed and typeset in Palatino Linotype by Indigo Dreams.
Front Cover: Design Ronnie Goodyer at Indigo Dreams
              The Glassblower photograph by Alison Hill
Printed and bound in Great Britain by: Imprint Academic, Exeter.

Papers used by Indigo Dreams are recyclable products made from wood grown in sustainable forests following the guidance of the Forest Stewardship Council.

CONTENTS

FOREWORD

At a first glance, the title *Poets in Person* may appear as not exceedingly original; it is, though, of particular significance to the participants in the present anthology. The history of the poetic encounter at The Glassblower Pub in London, May 2012, the incentive of this book, is a long one, but only a few facts will be mentioned here. It all started a few years ago with an amazingly fruitful dialogue at Prof. Lidia Vianu's *Translation Café* (Bucharest University), a dialogue that has owed much to George Szirtes and other British poets for their unparalleled involvement with students' literary translation work. In this context, I became acquainted with the creative platform *poetry p f*, a showcase of modern poets presented by Anne Stewart and featuring almost 300 writers with a great variety of styles and inspiration. Many of them were involved in the English – Romanian translation project *poetry pRO*, of which I was a member myself, and which inspired me to extend the idea to the German workshop of *the Dichthauer*, students of creative writing from the Ludwig-Maximilian University of Munich (LMU). That is how the project *poetry tREnD* came into existence, and a tremendous international exchange of poetry, translation work and, most important, friendship, began. This fruitful collaboration was crowned by the bilingual anthology *poetry tREnD* and the Literary Festival *W-ORTE*, organised by myself at the LMU in 2010. Eleven *poetry p f* poets joined this most successful and enjoyable event in Munich.

Another significant encounter took place a year later when I had the privilege to meet George Szirtes, whom I had admired and valued both as a poet and as a mentor in poetic and translational matters. A reading he gave at the LMU introduced him to the German students not only as a master of metaphors, but also as the same witty, unsophisticated, friendly person I had known at the *Translation Café*. An interview with him and his readiness to collaborate with my students in their endeavour to translate some of his poetry favoured a new fruitful cooperation.

Further virtual meetings turned into real ones. After several joint art and poetry projects with the poet and artist Steve Garside, Steve was invited to come and exhibit his photography at one of the photo exhibitions (2012) which I organise yearly at the LMU. In the same year, Alexandra Loske, tutor in art history at the University of Sussex, planned the launch of the anthology *Languages of Colour*, in which Steve and myself had some collaborative artwork. I took this as a good opportunity to meet some of the participants in the *poetry tREnD* project and, of course, George Szirtes, who was kind enough to accept my invitation. Though a bit sceptical at the beginning about the feasibility of getting together such a great number of poets (over 20), with the help of Anne Stewart and Rakesh Bhanot, the event called *Poets in Person* took place on a lovely sunny May day, and was both a high-level poetic encounter and a most enjoyable meeting of friends at The Glassblower Pub. A dream had come true, and needed a token that it had not been just a dream – hence the present anthology.

Here, I would like to thank all the participants who made this project possible and to express my gratitude to George Szirtes, who, besides offering some of his poems, honoured us with writing the Introduction to this book. Further thanks go to all those involved in the making of this book: to my son, Dorian, who took over the layout and the settling of all problems that arose during the editing process, and to Anne Stewart and Alison Hill, who kindly proofread the final version. As the editor of this book, I must say that I am happy and grateful to have met so many wonderful people IN PERSON.

Dr. Aprilia Zank

INTRODUCTION

In my craft or sullen art
Exercised in the still night
When only the moon rages
And the lovers lie abed
With all their griefs in their arms,
I labor by singing light…

Thus Dylan Thomas. The solitary art may be embarked on as a productive party game with others present, but even so it entails a withdrawal into the self as it experiences world and language at once, all its concentration focused on that imagined point from which poetry might spring. *If I knew where poems came from*, wrote Michael Longley, *I'd go there. Art is a house that tries to be haunted*, wrote Emily Dickinson. That singing light in the still night is its haunted home, but we can't enter it. We have to wait at its door. Nor do we always know where the house is, so we might immediately go there. But we want to find it, so we listen very hard, and after years of listening we may think we know the estate a little and may find the house. If only!

This is just a bunch of metaphors, but the evidence all points one way. We write alone, even when in company. We enter our listening selves alone.

But we need others to hear us. Maybe we need to know that others are listening, not only to us but to their equivalent of the source that feeds us. We need, from time to time, to feel the presence of fellow *makers*. Other writers are both companions and disturbance, just as we are to them. They are involved in the same madness, the same fixations, the same addiction.

And, at best, it is a kind of addiction. The reading of a poem may induce shivering, a change of breathing pattern, a quickening or slowing of the heart. It has physical effects. We need to be alone with it to experience it fully, but the poem wears its own loneliness, the best kind of loneliness, a loneliness where we are not on show, not acting within a social fabric, but are at some electrifying angle to the world.

In the end, of course, we do inhabit the social world and are inevitably part of the fabric. We get together with the like-minded and the prospectively like-minded – that part of humanity we recognise as having a discreet yet echoing existence – and we read our work and listen to others, listen despite the difficulties of concentration, despite the anxiety over our own performance in company, despite the vast, brilliant omnipresence of the external. We sit or stand and listen as best we can, assured only by others' listening, by the weight of words passing through our lips, proceeding from us, emanating from and re-entering language as spoken word, a brief pulse in time we have shaped into forms that may induce that quickening or slowing of the heart. We are an audience that is also a nest of singing birds. We are both self and metaphor.

This anthology, of which I am delighted to be a part, is that dual thing, a chorus full of solos. We drew together on a particular day to read to each other, and to others, and now here's the book. Starting with Baudelaire's pipe, the anthology moves through a rich range of colours: through "powder-blue sky", through "the yellow eye" and "too solid blue", ending with the "silver chime" of opening lilies. It is full of colour. The quality of work is high as it would be given the poets here. Many thanks to Aprilia Zank for that, for inviting me to be present and to write this brief introduction. It was a bright sunny day, a reasonable singing light.

George Szirtes

ANNE BERKELEY

Anne Berkeley won the first prize in the *TLS* competition in 2000 and was a prizewinner in the Arvon competition in 2004. She edited Rebecca Elson's acclaimed posthumous collection *A Responsibility to Awe* (Carcanet, 2001) and the poetry journal *Seam*. With the poetry ensemble Joy of Six, she has performed widely. Her first full collection, *The Men from Praga* (Salt, 2009), was shortlisted for the inaugural Seamus Heaney Centre Prize for best first collection.

What I like about the encounter with poetry from another language – whether it is in French, which I know a little, or through translation – is the challenge: that uneasiness of not knowing quite where you are, what the design of the street lamps will be, or the songs mothers sing to their babies. Sentence structure is different. The whole ambition of the poem can be different. There are things that can't be said in English. We avoid notions such as soul, heart, spirit. And when you don't know the source language, you have to take it all on trust and assume any strangeness is down to the original, without knowing how musical or conversational it is.

The sequence here is wholly dependent for its existence on Baudelaire's sonnet and my quarrel with it. If I am disrespectful it's because I take issue with its underlying nineteenth-century assumptions of privilege, but that I took the trouble at all is a measure of his enormous and continuing influence.

Baudelaire's pipe

I

Stroke
my Abyssinian hip:
I'm an experienced pipe –
a real writer's smoke.

When his spirits ache
my chimney fires up
like a home where good soup
greets the ploughman from work.

I embrace
and rock him idle
in my gauzy blue cradle,

whispering peace
in fragrant loops
from my passionate lips.

II

after Babelfish*

I am the pipe of a writer;
one sees, contemplating my mien,
Abyssinian or Cafrine,
that my master abuses his lighter.
When he's felled with pain,
I smoke like the cottage
where steaming pottage
awaits the homecoming swain.

I weave and I lull his soul
in the motile blue lace
that climbs from my mouth in fire,

and the powerful balm I roll
charms his spirit with grace
that lifts his heart from the mire.

(*Babelfish is an online automatic translation tool, named after
the fish in Douglas Adams's Hitch-hiker's Guide to the Galaxy)

III

I am the pipe of a writer;
you can tell from my complexion
he's held me in affection
since his teeth were whiter.

When he's feeling depressed
I'll be cooking the dinner
for the weary breadwinner
coming home for a rest.

I practise my charm
in flimsy blue laces,
with fragrant embraces,
and powerful balm
for the shift he must crave
from master to slave.

IV

I'm a writer's pipe
and I know my place,
my African face
his stereotype.

When his spirits droop
I'm the labourer's hut
where supper's hot
and I warm his lap,

then I tie him well
in lacy net
with a blue slipknot

and utter a spell
over my pet
in his oubliette.

V

I'm a poet's toke
tanned
in the hand
of an addict to smoke.

When things get him down
I'm the familiar chimney pot,
his something hot,
bath, slippers and dressing-gown.

I hold sway
in a blue
lasso

till he's well away,
off his face
in my embrace.

VI

I'm an author's pipe;
you can see from my face
the dominant race
buys that nicotine hype.

When he's feeling sore,
I pretend to cook
in a cosy nook
like a ganger's whore
and I rock his heart
in the blues I weave
when hot lips pucker

and my nebulous art

seems to relieve
the miserable fucker.

(published in *The Men from Praga*, Salt, 2009)

The men from Praga

Because my Polish doesn't run to 'tram ticket',
I have to walk. And my camera's jammed.
I jab it with my gloves. Brush at orange grit
the wind flings off the tarmac. It's miles.
And anyway, the light's gone.

Over the bridge, across the Vistula, is Praga –
the Bear Pit, the badlands, the concrete tower blocks.
The sky weighs down on the river, beats it flat,
squeezing out the scum that snags on reeds.
I imagine heavy industries upstream.

But it isn't scum. Ice. Its visible edge. Because,
down on the river, far from shore,
two men crouch on camp-stools, hauling
something in from the tricky gleam, doing
intricate, delicate things with their bare hands.

I watch them. They're quite at home
out there in the channel. Smoking, fixing bait.
The wind flicks Polish at me. It's all beyond me –
their Sunday morning ease, their ice,
the fluent fish at large below their feet.

(published in *The Men from Praga*, Salt, 2009)

DAVID COOKE

David Cooke started writing poetry in his late teens. In 1977, while he was still a student at Nottingham University, he won a Gregory Award and published his first collection, *Brueghel's Dancers* in 1984. He then stopped writing for over twenty years. His retrospective collection, *In the Distance*, was published in 2011 by Night Publishing, and a collection of more recent pieces, *Work Horses*, was published by Ward Wood Publishing in 2012.

His poems, translations and reviews have been accepted widely by journals including *Agenda, Ambit, The Bow Wow Shop, The Critical Quarterly, Cyphers, The French Literary Review, The Irish Press, The London Magazine, Magma, The North, Orbis, Other Poetry, Poetry Ireland Review, Poetry London, Poetry Salzburg Review, The Reader, The SHOp* and *Stand*.

Although I was brought up in the Southern English town of Reading, my family is Irish and as a child I regularly spent the long vacation on my grandfather's farm in Mayo. During those early years I had little doubt as to where my allegiance lay. I was unequivocally Irish and had no sense of being English at all, even though the way I spoke, for example, was quite different from that of my cousins. Making sense of my Irishness, or my lack of it, was what first got me into writing poems: nostalgic evocations of a rural paradise, but then, later, poems which were more questioning.

Equally problematical was my Catholicism or, again, my lack of it. However, it occurred to me recently that my early interest in languages and the fact that I studied French and German at university can be traced back to my fascination with the Latin text of the Mass. Although the service might seem interminable, I could always pass the time by matching the Latin to the English beside it. When, at the age of eleven, I went to a grammar school, I started to learn Latin properly and French, too. Eventually, I became a serial language learner: teaching myself German first and then, over time, dabbling in Italian, Spanish, Irish, Russian and many others – all of which, of course, I have found quite impossible to keep up with!

The poems I have chosen for this anthology are representative, in their different ways, of the kinds of influences I have sketched above. As a would-be rebel, I was also, sadly, a model student. In writing a poem about two French lovers from the 1940s it seems to me that I am reinventing the courtship of my parents. The 'anniversary' in the third poem looks back to France in the 1970s, where I worked as an English assistant and met my wife.

My take on van Gogh's masterpiece is informed by lapsed Catholicism and probably also by the work of the francophile Irishman, Samuel Beckett, whose plays and novels obsessed me in my late teens and early twenties.

Summer of '69

In the lightheaded lull
between exams
we lay at ease
among the roses.

Our striped ties
slackened off,
our top buttons
released,

we watched
bees returning
– like souls
from the underworld

we had glimpsed
in Virgil VI –
to Brother Simon's
flaking hives.

The previous year
in Paris students
had manned
the barricades;

while hair tucked
behind our ears,
or curled subversively
over collars,

we waged our own
secret war –
counting days
like sly insurgents.

The Lovers at the Bastille
after Willi Ronis

By the time they have reached
their vantage point they know
for certain that this is the day,
fixed in their memory
as their image is fixed in mine.

Across the city's foundering
skyline, its ramshackle roofs,
they see how in wintry light
Notre Dame is holding out
like an island under siege.

For a few moments longer
they'll stay, as one by one
beneath them shutters close
and the day's work ceases
in shops and ateliers.

Groomed for the afternoon
he has spent with her, he leans
over and whispers something
he has maybe said before –
some foolishness or a vow.

All we see of her is her back
in a tailored suit, her stance
and its hint of purpose. Knowing
the world for what it is
she will seek her place in it.

An Anniversary

Famous only for Rousseau's dreamy sojourn,
Chambéry lay huddled at the foot
of its calendar landscape, and there it was
we met, as if compelled
by a pattern in the lines on a map
to inhabit that region of mountains.

I wonder now do you still recall
our romantic isolation; how we grew familiar
with narrow streets so reticent and formal,
kept tidy as their own concerns;
cramped shops replete with goods
for a bustling clientele.

All that legendary summer we spent
our afternoons on the slopes
of St. Michel, making love
in a shimmering absence –
only the insects adrift in silence,
and the gliders above at a decent height.

After van Gogh

This is the room where a man sits alone
on a simple chair, his body slumped
in a pose of bleak interrogation,
his tunnel vision to see each work
as a chart of flawed intentions
his days locked in the bleared lens
of pointless despair, sensing too
beyond the flames of manic summers
that cold stars are turning,
tuned to a shrill monotonous note.

The Burgers of Calais

after Auguste Rodin

Connoisseurs of the smart move,
appraising the prices of commodities
and men, they stepped up against
their instincts, their futures anchored
in marriageable daughters,
the grit and astuteness of sons.

Their acquisitive eyes had once
been lit by the weight in tapestries
from Bruges or Ghent, the patience
entwined in filigree work or lace.
Solid tables sustained them.

Stripped here to a stark decency,
they are each wearing a halter
as they shuffle beyond
the starved confines of town.

Seeming defiant, one has stopped,
upright. Another cowers behind him.
Without recourse, all are abject –
bound only in the fellowship
of those reaching beyond their fear.

(published in *The London Magazine*, April/May 2013)

MARTYN CRUCEFIX

Martyn Crucefix has won numerous prizes including a major Eric Gregory award and a Hawthornden Fellowship. He has published five collections, including *An English Nazareth* (Enitharmon, 2004) and *Hurt* (Enitharmon, 2010). His translation of Rilke's "Duino Elegies" was shortlisted for the 2007 Popescu Prize for European Poetry Translation and hailed as "unlikely to be bettered for very many years" (*Magma*). His translation of Rilke's "Sonnets to Orpheus" was published in October 2012.

> *'The highest a man can attain is wonder, and when the primordial phenomenon makes him wonder he should be content.'* (Eckermann's *Conversations with Goethe*).

What Rilke calls praise, Goethe calls wonder and is best thought of as a partnership, a dance. But we are offered little choice but to live in times unpropitious to such dancing. Older traditions have long broken and who can escape a corrosive, wide-ranging scepticism on philosophical, moral and political issues? The success and dominance of scientific thought allows ever less room for traditional (and mistaken) ideas about absolute purpose or design. The result is our anxiety from the felt absence of something, fearing that we may be missing out on something we cannot even name. We crave distractions, the panorama of sights, sounds, thrills.

And all because the self is seen as an object over which the phenomenal flux of experience breaks in wave after wave. We are drawn to this image because experience includes memory and foresight, giving the impression that the self is something solid in the flow of time. Yet memory and anticipation are not of the essence, are mere corpses or fantasies of real experience. Like money they act only as promissory notes on the future or partial records of previous transactions. They are not the real presence of experience, not what Goethe calls the "primordial phenomenon".

The only way is to plunge in, move with the dance, the passionate measure. What we see with such a renovated vision is beauty and it can be through mimesis (by definition an attempt to blaze a trail into the full lucid presence) that the artist's self moves into congregation with the other. True mimesis counteracts the petrification of ideology, language and education to bring us into the lucid presence.

Poetry like this must take away solidity and turn beauty (which would otherwise be only statuesque and architectural) into a form more associated with music.

The truly open mind suspects even previously explored territory has not really been known. Most of us know instants when the beauty or strangeness of an ordinary scene draws the mind away from self-pursuit. We feel unable to find words, but poetry can express this as reminder, model and vicarious experience for its readers. The poet uses language to re-present experiences that are by definition ineffable using strategies such as mimesis, form, figurative and musical language. The poem suggests what cannot be plainly expressed. As Yves Bonnefoy says, poetry is not about something, but restores the self (ironically through language) to the full lucid intensity of experience, to an encounter with Goethe's "primordial phenomenon", to wonder.

Summerhouse

As the stream's bed is white and dry with dust
a billion leaves take the sunlight and shiver

with the vibration of insect life on all sides
the one ascending into the other's sphere –

this warmth unfolds round each vital thing
with this electric life of desire now you secure

drowned wings from a pool to dry in the sun
then look again and the air welcomes back

its gaudy fluttering – you watch as wings
go stumbling towards the lethal waters again

(commissioned/published for the *Magma* Poetry Competition
2012)

Water-lily

I

Mysterious – priapic – in her slow ascent
through olive-green, cloudy, particulate water.

Scarcely predicted, but looked-for for days,
her dark bomb rising, an old balancing act

on a turgid stalk. Upped in blind pursuit,
her slow-motion chasing out-riding scouts:

that series of pan-flat, broadening leaves
that wince red to racing green at the strain

of powering out of the pond's darkest places.
Imagined only by those who stoop low enough,

I see the crud, skeletal leaves, the sink away
to another dimension. Here at last she comes,

tracked close at four, three, two inches shy
of this world, seldom seen broaching herself

in the sun-warm air, the blue-lit afternoon.
In that instant becomes her own subject saying:

II

me, talk about me, about my tear-drop shape,
my split heart opening to kissable pink. Look!

Little raptor head! My dense-packed bud!
My elegant lack of interest in what lies ahead.

Out of this darkness, I leap to such climax,
to this ball-gown flounce I know is enough.

Not this distraught look, your agitated air.
Your stink. Your nice understanding! Talk!

Not your species' love of persecution –
no better reason than you mislike a face!

Not promises, cross-tongued, double-crossed,
all weakness, petty, knife-edged, taint.

Look how I rise – my focus, my intensity!
I am my own device. Then damn what's behind.

I give nothing of myself. All I want is free.
Shake off this idiocy! Take a look at me!

III

You stoop to find she cannot be still for long:
her surface beauty equivalent to being young.

You see the crud, skeletal leaves, the sink back,
say you've no reply to what she just said

since you carry such freight, so much baggage,
the worst and best of it your love of language.

Waiting like a spider at the cross-hairs
of words and things, you screw up in a moment,

lose it from paying too little attention,
from remaining shut tight in flesh and bone,

your eyes diminished with other men's dreams,
trying ideas, emotions like cast-off clothes.

You know little of yourself, less of others
but if once in a while the cross-hairs align,

straight, true, you say this, this is mine.
The report echoes long after the lily survives.

(published in *Hurt,* Enitharmon, 2010)

My brief career in medicine

This one believed I maybe had the brains
the other that I had the right demeanour

but the Schools denied me till it was too late
then reprieved me with the offer of a place

that by then I knew I could not refuse
such anticipation had struck such roots . . .

so I have no recall of the moment of choice
before those appalling digs in Eltham

where I stowed my dislocated skeleton
under the bed crammed one side of my head

with tendons muscles and pharmacol
with biochemistry bright nets of nerves

everything spilling from the other side
into failure – fallen to wandering streets

to stealing Everyman's Selected Wordsworth
I was John Stuart Mill in the hope my soul

would be saved while I felt love etiolating
the girl from home now a girl from home

her kisses like shrugs at London Bridge
saying go your own way at least not imposed

or not merely allowed if you want to live
deliberately then first you slit the shroud

(published in *The London Magazine,* Oct/Nov 2011)

MICHAEL CURTIS

Michael Curtis grew up in Liverpool, attended Oxford and Sheffield universities, worked in library and cultural services and managed poetry events and tours in the UK and abroad. He now lives in Kent. He is widely published in magazines and anthologies and has given readings, workshops and residencies in England, Ireland, France, Belgium, Finland, Latvia and Germany.

He was Writer in Residence for the Arts Council, England Great Expectations conference, the Metropole Arts Centre, Folkestone, the Maison de Poesie, Nord/Pas de Calais in France, and the Writers and Translators House, Ventspils, Latvia. His work has been studied and translated at the Universities of Liege, Bucharest and the Ludwig-Maximilian University, Munich and broadcast on radio in England, Ireland, Romania and Latvia. He has also assisted in translation from French, Finnish and Latvian.

His tenth poetry collection, *In the Affirmative*, was published in 2008 by Redbeck Press, *Walking Water*, an English/French sequence by Editions des Vanneux, appeared in 2009 and *Melnais suns*, Latvian translations of his poetry and prose, was published in 2010. *Horizon*, a collection of poems set on the Isle of Man, was launched in September 2012 at the first Manx LitFest.

Reaching beyond borders is in the nature of art. An international view of poetry crosses lines that need to be crossed. I enjoy reading poetry from other countries for the angles on life it offers, its arresting images, surprising technique, unusual subject matter and topography. This led me to collaborate with poets from other countries to organize tours and multinational events. My work has been translated into several languages, and discussion with translators always reveal hidden aspects and new insights. Physical and spiritual also interact during residencies abroad, most recently in Latvia, Germany, France and Belgium, where different cultural expectations and a welcome solidarity help to confirm the sometimes uncertain identity of writer.

Acoustics

Look into the distance
of your heart, eyes glazed
through a window fixed
on something or nothing
you pretend has seized
your complete attention,
appears to hold your gaze
when really the window
swings back on itself,
opens on a small interior
where you rehearse what
you'll say at the meeting,
replay that conversation
till you grab your chance,
disentangle the mess 4am
made of your mind, dream
of what you want to do
with the rest of your life, or
roll that morning's lyrics
around the perfect studio
hidden in your head,
compose unblemished solos
you'll never quite repeat
outside its unique acoustics
in echoing air, though
you try as often as you must,
conscious always of what
you lost, grateful always for
what you somehow found.

Disappearing

Slipping from volume
to silhouette till, dazzled
by sunrise, they disappear
behind forked trees
and let the morning swallow them.

This is all. And more, and quite
enough, the nurtured stuff
of winter dreams, dreamed
under stubborn greys that
wouldn't go away

unlike the sea, leaving
every day, the burnished pair,
new camera, striding
to the shore, an iridescent
swimsuit girl offering acrobatics

to the grateful sky. All will reappear
as light settles, staying bright
but not quite transparent
till evening's pinks and mauves
walk the waves again, a hammock

swings air to sleep, rubbed fronds
comfort themselves, cicadas
fill each softened ear, time
draws near, repeats its promise,
and I must disappear.

Last Names

In the popular charts
his polite Middle English
accomplished, refined
just pips her Old English
hewer of wood

little between them
like two children
heard in the same street
and called in for dinner
ten doors apart.

But even the same one
signed in the register
when they set up home
didn't keep them together
when his was called

until hers could depart
all those years later
to leave me unanswered
by careful inscriptions
on slivers of metal

that strain to be heard
in the competing crush
of memorial rose beds
cluttered with blossom
and deafened by hearts.

One Morning

One morning, much like any other,
they let themselves in, uninvited.
Had you guessed they were there,
waiting outside, in all weathers, from
time to time rattling the door
or trying a back window?

One morning, much like any other,
they marched down the hall
and straight into the kitchen
where you sat folding the paper,
looking up as they entered your head
and took every memory

in a single flash of forgetting.
I asked you something,
what was on television today,
something like that, I can't recall,
and you hadn't a clue. What I'd said.
Where you were. Who you were.

One morning, unlike any other,
they stole your fierce opinions,
the faces of your children,
the sound of your own voice. Left you
waiting inside, whatever the weather,
for the authorities to find them.

Complete

The drum of your ear beats
a rhythm for my heart. Arms
fold supplication. Your heat
blankets my chest, begs
questions of love - limits
we'll never touch. Legs ascend
to circle me as small alarms
rock the cradle of your spine.

Fingers clench, chord dreams
for orchestras to rehearse
under spotlight stars. Driven
forward, each day discovers
continents, crosses oceans.

I sit at your perfect feet.

MARTINA EVANS

Martina Evans is a poet and novelist. She grew up in County Cork, the youngest of ten children. She is the author of nine books of prose and poetry. Her fourth poetry collection, *Facing the Public*, was a TLS Book of the Year in 2009 and won the Premio Ciampi International Prize for Poetry in 2011. 'Petrol', a prose poem won a Grants for the Arts Award in 2010 and was published by Anvil Press in 2012. 'Through The Glass Mountain', a new dramatic poem, was published by Bloom Books in June 2013.

One needs solitude to write poetry, only then can one hear the voices from that haunted house of which Czeslaw Milosz reminds us in his great poem, Ars Poetica; our house is always open/ there are no keys in the doors,/ and invisible guests come in and out at will. And these poems written in the space of solitude can't really exist until they cross those invisible borders again to reach their readers.

Kept Back

Prayer, the last refuge of the scoundrel
                              Lisa Simpson

Even Bart Simpson felt the shame,
yellow and unreal as he was and
everything distracted him but especially
the snowstorm that God sent – he slumped
slogging over a book while everyone
in Springfield linked arms in a circle,
singing *A Winter Wonderland.*
But I was good at reading. I'd gone
through the library and back, it was all
inside me, how the Japanese houses
were made of paper in case of
Earthquake and Eskimos lived
in igloos made of bricks of solid ice
and the length of a boa constrictor
was as long as six boys with American
crew cuts, wearing turned-up jeans on
six bicycles. The prayers were
only an afterthought - didn't we say them
every day until we were sick of them?
The colours of the Ladybird fairy tales scorched
on my brain, Cinderella's three dresses, blue and
pink and gold and roses and the Elves
and the Shoemaker, blue and green and pink with
gold boots and the Ugly Duckling.
                              I didn't hear

that it was my mother's decision
until years later when someone said
Mrs McCarthy didn't speak to her for a week.
My mother who revered teachers,
crossing words over this one?
She, who told them not to spare the rod?

All I knew then was what I heard,
the others stumbling over
their Acts of Faith, Hope and Charity,
I was so sure that I knew the Acts only
the teacher's finger pointed straight.
No First Holy Communion for me.
I would never be sure again.
Even Bart managed to woo Miss Krabappel
into giving him a D minus in the end and
he passed into fifth grade.
But I was kept back and that was a Godless
yellow feeling, repeating
outside the ring of First Holy Communion dresses
that went round and round,
white and crisp as a Winter Wonderland.

Supervised Study

Eugie gets off her high chair
at the top of the study and paces
between our desks, Sister Mary
Eugenius has the bluest eyes and
she walks like a man, like she's never
cared for her own good looks.
She puts the fear of God
in the girls yet she likes me, thinks
I'm good at French. Her subject.
Four brown-papered textbooks
are carefully arranged in what I call a *quad*
over Mario Puzo's *The Godfather*.
I jolt when she pauses by my desk,
attracted by *French Verbs*
ostentatiously displayed on the left.
On top, another textbook, *Maupassant*.
Once, Guy was another secret read,
resting on my knees under the desk
with one eye on the Master. At ten,
the weirder the story, the better
I liked it but I've moved on to the
Sicilians. Eugie groans with delight
as she plucks Maupassant, from the desk,
Quelle histoire? Ah Vendetta –
tres interressant! I blush, it must
have passed for shyness,
The Godfather is nakedly displayed
on my desk but she does not see it.
Eugie's glad, she tells me, to see
I'm finally settling down
making full use of my God-given ability.

Vocation

I was always afraid
the Virgin Mary would speak
to me. Wasn't she always
appearing to lowly types
that no one believed in and that
were reviled by the whole world?
I didn't think my heart
could stand it if God
thought I was a candidate.
Once in Burnfort, the
muffled sound of a car
behind me was like wings
rushing and the headlights
beamed from behind as
I knelt in the snow with head
bowed and the Cortina passed
on. I cringed for years after.
During our final exams
I told Sister Therese
and Therese, thrilled, rushed
to the head nun before
I could stop her
announcing my vocation.
I stood beside her in Regina Caeli,
the senior dormitory
with the big single rooms where, significantly I
had never been given one,
cringing again
as she told Sister Benedicta who
taught me Geometry and once said
I was *the boldest girl in the school*,
that my *whole life*
was a brazen act.
Benedicta's outsize grey eyes

were opaque now with suspicion and
poor Therese trembling
as if she is before God
the two of us like fools
as Benedicta slowly pronounced
Oh is that so?

Anatomy Lesson

I've still got my *head in the books*
sucking the clandestine comforts.
I'm twenty and Professor Coakley
jerks his knee like a whip of rope
demonstrating muscle movement
at the top of the class. It's *Tess*
this time on my desk in another *quad*
- *Kitty Clark's Positioning* and others.
Oh Thomas Hardy is morbid enough
for me, all right and when the girls sit
forward, I know I'm missing something
interesting about muscles or is it tendons?
I'm sure now that I'm *doomed* to be always holding
the wrong book. The pretty Opus Dei celibate
struggles excitedly through the door with
the rattling skeleton, *Oh Professor Coakley!*
She is called a Numerary and
there are rumours she wears a spiked chain
around her thigh. On top, she is definitely wearing
a desert-coloured Prada sweater, her hair
cut in a perfectly symmetrical shining
brown cap, her face deeply red
before the distinguished Professor and
I hate the way the other girls
look at her, smile and exchange looks.

Flowers in the Attic

I hate Dublin and the radiography lectures
and the X-ray department even more,
they laugh at my Cork accent and one
of them said *Aids is a North Side disease.*
I don't want to be here with the snobby girls
with the Donnybrook accents or the registrar
who has nick-named me *Cork* even though
he is kind. The girl who loves sailing
asks every single one of us what our fathers
do – owning a pub
sounds like something dirty now.
Alone for a moment, I crawl into the shower
with *Flowers in the Attic* and a cinema-sized
bag of Maltesers. Minutes later, Sister
Patricia taps on the door. She smiles
at her fellow Corkonian. I know she cycles
the underground corridors of St. Vincent's
in the dark evenings, her white veil flying.
I know she knows a fellow oddball.
Now, Tina.
I hide my trashy book behind my back.
*When you've wiped your face, you'll
have to come back to Nuclear Physics.
The Siemens engineer's been in there
for the last five minutes.* I'm nearly twenty-one
scared I'm pregnant,
no qualifications, no hope yet
mournfully following her white habit.

That's Entertainment

My mother describes the emigration:
Expensive full fares for the whole family
when we could have all gone for ten pounds
on the Australian government. The fools
we were and Nuala and Mary getting up,
non-stop to sing and Mary entertaining
the whole ship for weeks with talk. I think
of my mother's mantra, *For God's sake,*
take your head out of the books and talk
to the customers. Ber tells me how
she remembers Tricia in a rage
when I wouldn't *hop to it*
despite the funeral crowd pouring
down the road, a black mass
of relentless figures, hurrying to our door.
How Tricia flung *Vanity Fair* across the red
and white and blue tiled floor and the other
book lover, Pats Curtain noticed me,
the way I ran after the book *to mind it first*
before I attended to the customers and
he said that I carefully marked my page.

(all poems are from the collection *OH BART*, Rack Press, 2012)

STEVE GARSIDE

Steve Garside is an artist, photographer and writer from Rochdale, Lancashire. He has exhibited his creative work in Europe and the UK, and has been published in UK, USA and Europe. He has written much poetry for charitable events and has facilitated poetry workshops and writing groups. Steve has been involved in many creative writing projects and exhibitions.

Poetry is for me, about recording moments of time and thought. Each poem reflects the emotional space of the poet at the time of writing, and central to the life of the poem is the use of metaphor; that being used within the sensory aspects of the collective words of the poem.

Meeting as well as reading the work of other writers is an illuminating experience. The rhythms within languages, cultural understandings and the subjective perceptual influence on the written word and thought I find to be a magical experience in terms of social learning and humility.

Poetry transcends us all, and I am very grateful to be resting within the pages of this anthology. It is my sincere hope that my journey to this point might inspire others to expend their singular skills into the writing of poetry.

Family

She wore a monochrome smile
and an out-of-date sweater,
his eyes betrayed the fact
that someone else was looking in,
the only image they could find of her
was the one with the grainy sun.

His was taken in the shush of a booth
while the rest of the living were shopping,
the children's pictures;
knot-tied, combed and blazered,
cheeks flushed of the morning,
their nan's; her last passport pic
while someone's baby looked beyond the lens.

Glasses on in middle age
circled in a muddle of mates,
a black and white girl
fully dressed on a grey beach,
a missing son in a stranger's yard,
a gun, a blade – a flicker of bone,
a second, a whisper; the word.

Visiting Rights

He sits, matchstick clean
corner flat, curtains drawn
single man, waiting.
He lets me in with a sigh
I spy no laptop
daylight kitchen hiss
his dado rail is spotless.

He twitches to offer me tea
fluff seeds satellite space
supernovae silence remains.

A single cable snakes
from a hollow box
which pulses to the pause
of my unanswered eye –

and in all those other rooms
courtships slip
cortex from cortex
fever licked – synapse slick;
synopsis of its own continent.

She asked for it he tells me,
she asked for it that oversexed bitch.

signs
(for Marianne Daniels)

I open as spring
in a country you find
familiar as the vowels
on your fingertips.

Counting seconds
three and five
we synchronise streets
with measures of time,
drape white sheets
over old broken houses,
find string for bunting
and tin can telephone calls;

the party's about to start,
please bring your friends –
tell them all to come
to the roof of this moment
and smile; just smile.

Tidal Flow
(for Faraj Bayrakdar)

There is a space.
A space which sleeps between
this seeping becoming of words
and bristling grass of afternoons.
The space which hits this auditorium of dark
flecked light of time with fingernail tallies
and the hanging gift outside.

I wear the promise of my skin,
I am the numb of numbers –
in silence there's no breath
for questions.

Poem

Had I the eye to carve marble –
To stiffen my wrist; fist grip a chisel
To sculpt the script of my heart for you
I would, with my imagination taut
As a cello bow, draw out this sky
We sit beneath smiling,
And be the lilting kiss of grass
Where we gift our words of love
For others to cherish in the well
Of a given tear; for death masters all.
Let me set my beating task like a man
Willing music into the chambered kernel
Of his own craft not once before kissed
Full sail by the night measure of himself
So soon becoming whispered cemetery of days.
For I am the cooling land from your arrival
and each word arrow sent from ever –
I am my spent art of stone flecks showering
this ground crowned statue of you.

Note found on the table

It's old news of course
Up at 6am to write
Not a sound except
Those birds
Whose generations
Twirl their incessant
Song each morning
Yet to prove its worth.

Never is there a moment
When one generation
Laments the last –
Nor dawn march of doves
Or biscuit crumbs
To litter this lawn of words.

Never has something
Been written so true
Whilst becoming 6am.

Today

the school drop off –
the last minute finding out about
the fresh painted double yellow lines
where we usually park to chat
before the bell,
the line up, the waving goodbyes –
the 'have the best day ever kisses'.

Don't wait; move on with life
through green turning amber –
an old horse in a misty field,
a fading speed sign –
streets becoming
impervious to rainwater,
dragooned it seems from
moving clouds not waiting
for any line painted;
nor any final waving away.

CECELIA GRANT-PETERS

Cecelia Peters grew up and still lives in Langley, Berkshire, with her two sons. She is a Paralegal and started writing poetry at the age of about seven. In her teens she was a member of Slough Writers' Group, later in her twenties she joined the West London Writers' Guild. As a student at Langley College in the 1970s she was a contributor to their magazine 'Info 'and also Editor of a teenage magazine for Orchard Youth Club in Slough 'Scene One.' She has had numerous poems published in magazines and newspapers, and on local radio, and is currently working on her third book, *The Rage in Albion* after the poem of the same name. She is also the author of *Words Is What I'm Doing* and *The Muse*. She regularly performs her work on stage at The Firestation in Windsor, Berkshire.

Cecelia also tutors a children's poetry workshop for the London based charity, Kids Company, which she currently uses in many schools and libraries. She is also one of the Judges for the Royal Berkshire Poetry Competition, and a regular contributor to online Magazines, *Glow* and *Beat*.

Cecelia's poetry is stark and uncompromising, and unlikely to appeal to those who like moons in June and happy endings. Many of her poems are observational based on characters she has encountered throughout her life. Many are spiritual and romantic and are based on nature. She does not mince her words and gets straight to the point and often refers to herself as the "No Holds Bard."

I enjoy writing about people, but there is always a little bit of me in each rhyme. Most of the rhymes are based on real people whom I have met, or on my own or their personal experiences. For example,

'The Mountain' is based on a friend's story of his journey to Kenya where he met a group of people from all walks of life. He was intrigued by the feeling of well being and how well everyone got on. He mentioned the amazing mix of flora and fauna and I thought they sounded better with their Latin names.

My most famous poem 'The Rage in Albion' is an observation of my encounter with a curious and enigmatic "homeless man under the bridge", whose placards have become his voice, so far read by over 200,000 people. Thrillingly dark and evocative, my aim is to uplift the reader giving a feeling of awe and enchantment, then gradually down to stark reality.

The Rage in Albion

The homeless man under the bridge had eyes that bled
And woke each night from his humble bed
He had no poetry or rhyme,
No joy, no consequence or crime.
He wanted only food and bed,
And spoke of Albion with fear and dread.

He held a placard with words that read:
"ENGLAND IS A PLACE OF WOE AND DREAD,
A COUNTRY OF NO LAW OR GRACE
ENGLAND IS A DREADFUL PLACE."

The Poet asked his name, and the homeless man said:
"I am the Rage in Albion, I have no name
For I am England's burden, and I am England's shame,
Mark my visage, Mark my frown
I am the Rage in Albion
I rise when the sun goes down
And when the single mother weeps on the other side of town
There will be Rage in Albion when the sun goes down".

The Homeless man under the bridge held a placard that read:
"ENGLAND IS A PLACE OF WOE AND DREAD,
A COUNTRY OF NO LAW OR GRACE
ENGLAND IS A DREADFUL PLACE."

Again, the Poet asked his name, and the homeless man said:
"I am the Rage in Albion, Poet do not weep
I lay wake at night whilst Albion is asleep,
My eyes once blue are now blood red,
I am the Rage in Albion, the living who are dead
And when the Poet weeps with sadness on the other side of Town
There will be Rage in Albion when the sun goes down".

The Homeless man under the bridge held a placard that read:
"ENGLAND IS A PLACE OF WOE AND DREAD,
A COUNTRY OF NO LAW OR GRACE
ENGLAND IS A DREADFUL PLACE."

He looked me in the eye and said;
"Poet, do not weep,
I only rise when Albion is asleep
My burdens they are many but my heart is strong
And I roam in the night for the days are too long
Mark my visage, Mark my frown
I am the Rage in Albion
I rise when the sun goes down."
And when a little child goes hungry on the other side of town
There will be Rage in Albion when the sun goes down."

The Homeless man under the bridge held a placard that read:
"ENGLAND IS A PLACE OF WOE AND DREAD,
A COUNTRY OF NO LAW OR GRACE
ENGLAND IS A DREADFUL PLACE".

(published In *Beat*, April 2011)

The mountain

Imams offer prayers to Allah
As Minarets chant high
Rastafarians invoke Tafari
And chant down Babylon
Locals smoke Bang in the Siesta
Sages chant Mantras as
Holy men speak incantations
Christians filled with the Holy Ghost
Weep with joy and gladness
Dalits are "touchable"
Anything is possible on the mountain.
Stars like diamonds ornament the sky
Flora and fauna shelter in the moonlit escape
Beauty is prevalent on the mountain
Primula Vulgaris
Iris Germanica
Viola Alba
Acacia Fania
Narcissus Poeticus Poeticus
Lamu

The woman who lived inside her head

There was a woman who lived inside her head
She daily spoke to the people
Who lived inside her head
Outside her head the world continued
Outside her head the band played on
Outside her head the parties were in full swing.
There was a woman who lived inside her head
A passerby approached her and he said;
Aren't you the woman who lives inside your head?"
She charged the wise old LADY who
Told her stories of her life before
She occupied her space inside her head
She loved the MAN who hugged her..... inside her head
He regularly held her hand and esteemed her,
But only for a short time.....she said
For he was the MAN who encouraged
The woman who lived inside her head.
There was a woman who lived inside her head
Outside her head the people went along with their business
Outside her head NURSES charged about, and DOCTORS
                                        prodded,
ORDERLIES were disorderly..... and then the woman
Retreated back inside her head.
Meanwhile on the outside life continued
But.... at a slower pace,
The moon shone ....but brighter
The seas rose, kingdoms fell and wars raged
But still the woman continued to live inside her head.
The people on the OUTSIDE told her she was "Mad" or "Bad"
                                        and even "Dead"
But "NO" she said, "I am NOT Mad, or Bad or even Dead
I simply choose to live inside my head".

**Sarah's Song
or, Girl Interrupted**

Oh her shoes are shiny and her hair is long
And she sings the mighty Sarah's Song
Oh Sarah's Song is a song of rage
With themes she learnt from an early stage
She has no formal education
But she has sheer determination

She's a girl interrupted.

She was gravely used at the age of six
By a Fiend who taught her Adult tricks
So Sarah's Song was a song of rage
With themes acquired at an early age
When the dark days came and the nights of pain
She composed herself with a bold refrain.
Even though what occurred was oh so wrong
She consoled herself with a constant song
And her song was borne out of constant rage
And the strength acquired at an early age

It's been thirty years since that fateful day
When a Fiend took Sarah's joy away
But she overcame and she triumphs still
With a constant song and an iron will.
For she kept on walking and she did not die
And she mocked the Fiend who made her cry
As a girl interrupted she had no rights – then
She was Angry, Hurt, and she Hated men

But she ran from her jail and she now is – free
And she knows she can no longer – be

A girl interrupted

Oh her shoes are shiny and her hair is long
And she keeps on singing Sarah's Song
Now Sarah's Song is a song of praise
With themes she learnt from most recent days
She escaped her jail and she now is – free
And she knows she can no longer – be

A girl interrupted.

(published in *The Muse*, April 2010)

ALISON HILL

Alison Hill's pamphlet, *Peppercorn Rent*, was published by Flarestack in 2008, and a full collection, *Slate Rising*, was published in 2014 by Indigo Dreams Publishing. Her work has appeared in a wide range of magazines and anthologies, and 'To a Girl on Platform Three' was nominated for the Forward Prize. Alison founded and runs Rhythm & Muse, a monthly music and poetry night at the Ram Jam Club in Kingston on Thames. R&M celebrated its fifth anniversary in 2012 with the launch of *Lyrical Beats*, edited by Alison, which features the work of more than fifty poets and musicians.

Alison was the first Poet in Residence at Kingston Libraries (2011-12) and ran a series of events and workshops for adults and children. She also writes plays and her first script, *Stalking Oscar*, was staged at the cornerHOUSE, Tolworth, in 2008.

Alison lives next to Bushy Park in Teddington, Middlesex.

Writing is generally a solitary activity, so readings and events are invaluable for sharing work and getting away from the pen and keyboard. Having run Rhythm &Muse for six years, I appreciate how important it is for writers to meet regularly. I can recall most R&M nights and many other poetry events I've been to over the years; there's an essential element of mixing with other writers and sharing creative energy. The Glassblower gathering was in a sun-filled room, Irish music wafting up from the street below, with poetry, chat, food and drink – a perfect combination.

To a Girl on Platform Three

She knows she's young enough and cool enough
    to wear
a short lilac dress with a cropped leather jacket,
    glossy hair
streaming back from flawless skin.

She's intent on texting, ignoring the sun flaring at
    her feet,
pooling her moments of pure, incandescent youth.
I see her in years to come, when she finds the
    dress
tossed at the back of her wardrobe, as she smiles
in fleeting recognition and passes it on.

Lilac sucks, her daughter thinks, but she takes it
    politely,
as the sun dapples around her varnished feet.

(published in SOUTH 45 and *Lyrical Beats*, September 2012)

Valley Woman

Hands on hips
broadening over the valley
she surveys the impasse:
can she leap, will he follow?

Eyes narrowed, dark squint
lessening the load,
she takes the plunge
and makes it to the other side,
just one damp underskirt
to show for her leap of faith.

He had less belief,
raging on the river bank,
helpless and impotent
as the river surged
and swallowed him whole.

She walked on with a shrug
and two dry stockings.

Artful Dodgers

We whitewash our walls
then sit and wait
for the perfect picture
to find its perfect space.

Sometimes it works
and the room is complete
with one hammer and two nails.

Other times the plaster
takes a beating,
nails go in and out
and pictures spend time
in limbo, leaning casually
against a radiator,
canvas to canvas
against another scene
that's waiting
for the just the right spot.

One day I found the walls bare:
the art had left home,
frame behind frame,
and settled snugly
along our neighbours'
rose-splattered walls,
smug and over-crowded,
nailed to perfection.

Tapestry Lines

She spotted them in dusty antique shops,
absently tracing intricate coils
on fading patterns.

Texture of childhood, she could feel
the music swell, smooth red wine
shivering down the glass.

She fingered the fabric again, pulled
the tapestry away from its lay line,
laid bare a new skin.

Her new family drew close, smiling
expectantly as she lifted the lid
and the notes flew out.

She pulled them closer, heard only the music.

Water Lies Heavy

(After the Vestal Virgin Tuccia
Giovanni Battista Moroni, c.1555)

She carries water in a sieve
or so the story goes, yet she knows more,
knows that when she rises to her swollen feet
the water will seep into her toes,
dispelling the myth of her
misplaced virginity.

For all those feet clicking past,
all those eyes over the centuries,
all those people who have swallowed
what is written by her side, in miniature,
believe what her maker wants them to believe:
Chastity emerges from the dark clouds of infamy

She smiles in complicity as we move on.

(published in *Snakeskin* 181, November 2011)

Crushed Velvet

She pushed at the space between words,
trying to fathom her place among
the shimmering constellations.

He'd promised her the earth that night
and the next few after that, stray whispers
gathering at the edge of darkness.

The flash of dawn disturbed her every time,
as he stole her senses one by one,
pressed stars upon her mind.

By the next morning he was passing
the marmalade in silence, only looking up
when his father entered the room.

She'd longed to touch the velvet falling
at his wrist, trace the curls around his cuff
with a slender, timid finger.

He rebuked her with a nonchalant air,
a smile of indifference and marked absence
of any backward glance.

That was fifty years ago, if not more, yet still
she pushed the walls, the door, the space
between, asking to be let in.

(shortlisted/commended in the Grace Dieu Writers'
Competition 2013)

KAVITA JINDAL

Kavita Jindal is the author of the critically-acclaimed poetry collection *Raincheck Renewed* published by Chameleon Press in Hong Kong. She also writes literary criticism and fiction. Her short story, 'A Flash of Pepper', won the Vintage Books/Foyles 'Haruki Murakami competition' in January 2012. Kavita's work has appeared in literary journals, anthologies and newspapers around the world including *The Independent, The South China Morning Post, The Indian Express, Dimsum, The Mechanics' Institute Review, Asia Literary Review, Cha, The Moth Magazine, In Our Own Words,* and *Not A Muse.* Recent poems have appeared in *The Yellow Nib* edition of *Modern English Poetry by Indians* (July 2012, Belfast, UK); the *HarperCollins Book of English Poetry* (July 2012, New Delhi, India) and the *Lyrical Beats* anthology (Autumn 2012, London, UK).

Kavita's poems have been translated into Arabic, German, Punjabi and Romanian, and some poems have been adapted to be set to music.

She was born in India and lived in Hong Kong for many years before settling in London. Her work draws on the heritage of many lands.

It is always a joy to come together in a gathering of poets and spend some hours immersed in the poetry of other voices and other perceptions. The rare day of London heat, the reunion of the poets from the W-Orte festival in Munich and the addition of guest performers made The Glassblower readings in May 2012 special. Consciously or unconsciously we learn much from listening to poets reading their own work and if they hail from disparate parts of the globe, so much the better. A poetic encounter is an opportunity to expand our horizons.

     In this anthology I have included the three poems I read at The Glassblower, for the simple reason that they illustrate my writing inspirations and my word-collector's instinct of pulling together random strands from journeys and experiences to fuse into a poem. 'Aljez At Midnight' was written in Eagle Bay, Western Australia; 'A Bonsai for Princess Masako' was written in Kyoto, Japan; and 'It Was in May. The Sky Poured.' was transcribed in London but set in the memory of a rainstorm in South India.

It was in May. The sky poured.

The day the gutters overflowed
I left Kotapuram Port.

Abandoned on the platform were black trunks and tan suitcases
forsaken to their drenching while the porters huddled
under the whipped red awning.
The long brown train awaited the flutter of the guard's green flag
as with slick-wet hair, from the window I stared
at a shadow I thought was there.

Friends wrote after long silences to say they'd told you
I'd shed tears on a platform awash with water
Scraped on to the train and cried again.
It was too good not to repeat.
You were puzzled when you heard this
or that's the version I received.

It wouldn't have changed anything, you said
if you'd been there, if you'd spoken
It wouldn't have erased the train timetable
or the date of leaving Kotapuram
If you'd said 'best of luck in life, my friend'
or another farewell equally inane
I'd have lived exactly the life I have
it would all have panned out the same.
I would've left on the day the sky poured
the day the gutters overflowed
Even if you'd stood there
to say 'Hello. Goodbye. I care.'

'Tears?' you'd asked, with perplexed brow when the story
                                      was repeated
of rampant lightning and umbrellas twisted by the storm.
Of the face squelched to the streaky window.

- 73 -

'Tears, for what purpose?'

There were pillars on the platform
Posters on the pillars, imploring us to
Stick No Bills
The yellow of the posters was shiny-succulent, water-lashed.
The pillars were white and round, the sodden green flag was down,
the train slipped out, pulled away my stare,
away from the shadow I thought was there.

It was in May. The sky poured. The gutters overflowed.
I left Kotapuram behind. The trains ran on time.

(published in *The Yellow Nib edition of Modern English Poetry by
Indians,* 2012, U.K., and the *HarperCollins Book of English Poetry,*
2012, India)

Aljez at midnight

I try to speak to her but she ducks backwards into
                                    the moon-drenched cave
Called under the duvet
It is where loops loop, corkscrews take the first turn,
                                    lyrics hunt for melody
Or become babies' rattles

'I was thrown,' she says, 'thrown into the arum lily marshes
Like a discarded baby's rattle
Complete with first bite marks, indentations on red plastic
Hidden jangly bells

'Arum lilies absorbed me as I sank
Lifted their proud heads to the sky
Their fluted petals tight and mysterious gave nothing away
To light or dark
To silence or sound'

I try to speak to her, crawling forwards into
                                    the moon-drenched cave
Called under the duvet
It is where loops loop, corkscrews take the first turn,
                                    babies' rattles are sown
In arum lily marshes.

(published in the *HarperCollins Book of English Poetry*, 2012,
India)

- 75 -

A Bonsai for Princess Masako

In the imperial garden
Chrysanthemums grow
Take their places
Know their roles

Gardeners' gloves
Watering cans
Fertilizers

Got her down

Alive in Spring?
As far as we know
Bright, blossoming?
Not as before

Precious teasing
Pruning clippers
Weed killers

Got her down.

(published in *The Yellow Nib edition of Modern English Poetry by Indians*, 2012, U.K.)

Anything but

On Not Being a Muse

I will write it
And if you like
I will sing it

I will arrange it, strum it
Pick it, drum it

I will edit it, compress it,
Finesse it, billboard it

I will design it, knit it,
Dye it, fit it

I will brushstroke it, pleat it
Murmur philosophy beneath it

Gladly I will do it all
Anything but be
Static while you are active
Anything but be
The one from whom you draw
What you make your own.

(commissioned for the anthology *Not A Muse*, 2009, Hong Kong)

Patina

I have wrapped up the hurt
like a betel nut in a betel leaf
sugared it
tucked it under a stone

There's no weeping to show for it
Under the stone
the sugar melts
runs red with betel juice

Stripping and polishing the core
Giving it patina
to be appreciated
by a collector of antiques.

(published in *The Lamp & Owl*, Birkbeck, 2005, London, and
 in *Private –International Review*, 2005, Italy)

ALEXANDRA LOSKE

Alexandra Loske is an art historian, curator and editor with a particular interest in late eighteenth and early nineteenth century European art and architecture. She was born and grew up in Germany and moved to England in 1997, where she first worked as a bookseller in London's Charing Cross Road. She has been working at the University of Sussex since 1999 in various roles. Since 2008 she has been researching the use of colour in the Royal Pavilion in Brighton, the Regency holiday palace of King George IV. Alexandra is also the managing editor of the Frogmore Press, which publishes a literary journal and other collections.

Picking from the rainbow: On editing *Languages of Colour*

In May 2012 I edited and published an anthology entitled *Languages of Colour*, comprising poetry, prose, critical writing and art work on the theme of colour. The title might suggest a discussion of linguistic aspects of colour, but in this context 'languages' stands for the many different approaches and attitudes to colour and how colour is used as a tool in various art forms and disciplines, just as actual languages vary and interact with each other. Serendipitously, languages in a non-metaphoric sense found their way into the collection, with one French poem and translations from French and German. I am an art historian and a few years ago I embarked on doctoral research into colour schemes and the use of pigments in historic interiors, so it was only natural that I wanted to emphasise the strong link between the visual and decorative arts and creative writing. The anthology would therefore include a large number of colour illustrations, a range of historical images and contemporary artwork. I had been quietly hoping that my call for submissions would result in at least a few direct collaborations of artists and writers or poets, and I was also simply curious to see and read how exactly colour was used by writers as a tool or an inspiration. The response to the call for submissions was as varied in form and focus as I had expected, and more overwhelming than I had anticipated.

At the outset I had the rather naïve idea of organising the anthology neatly in the Newtonian order of rainbow colours. The originality of the submissions and the infinitely creative nature of both language and colour soon made it clear to me that this could not be achieved and that instead I should let the book express exactly this. So there is no division between fiction and non-fiction, poetry and prose, image and text, nor is there a chronological order. I tried to let the pieces connect and speak to each other as seemed natural. The result is an anthology that includes pieces as diverse as an essay on a sixteenth century Italian colour dictionary, a poem on the fear of yellow, musings on the wrong kind of blue in the sky of early photographs, notes from a library devoted to colour and two different translations of Rimbaud's famous colour poem *Voyelles*.

However, reading and re-reading the submissions I noticed that certain themes and notions began to stand out; some of them expected, some less so. Colour is, if you want, an abstract concept and well as an abstract substance, making it extremely malleable in poetic as well as visual terms. You can admire the blue in a Titian sky, a medieval stained glass window or in Vermeer's interiors, which might lead to thoughts about the value of the various pigments used to create these objects and images, thus perhaps explaining symbolic value associated with certain colours. Is pigment an abstract material, you might wonder, contemplating a thimbleful of ground lapis lazuli from deepest Afghanistan, a pigment that, a few hundred years ago, was more expensive than gold, was given a name that was at once descriptive and poetic, *Ultramarine*, meaning 'from across the sea'. From here you could move on to abstract art and consider what links the precious ultramarine pigment to artists who made colour the subject of their art, such as Rothko, Gerhard Richter or, perhaps most famously, Yves Klein, who was determined to invent his own blue, *International Klein Blue*, and, when he had succeeded, appeared to be dyeing his whole world blue.

In poetry, the abstract quality of colour and the largely un-systemised and therefore wonderfully arbitrary naming of colours mean that it has been used by poets as tool and metaphor throughout history, and occasionally colour and pigments themselves are the topic of poetry, or at least its starting point. A poet might link pigment references to a painting, the creative process of producing a work of art, or invoke a particular phase in the history of material culture. In the *Languages of Colour* anthology this is achieved to notable effect in Tamar Yoseloff's poem *Illumination*, which paints a picture (excuse the pun) of a medieval scribe's workshop in a few carefully crafted lines, beginning with a list of painting materials:

> Gold leaf, cadmium, ochre, saffron –
> indelible once set on vellum.
>
> The monks ground azurite and lapis
> for perfect blue, took care
>
> to cleanse their hands of poison
> that made words sacred.
> […] (Loske, 2012: 33)

Similarly, James Goodman conveys the joy of using and naming material colour in his poem *Painting the Clay*:

[...]
white with a hint of clitter on the sea-ward moor
white with a hint of clatter of falling rocks
tiny white with a shadow of slow wing turning
bone white with a blush of clay marrow
[...] (id.: 12)

Colour as such, as a great abstract and at times non-material entity, gives poets a large playing field, and a number of submissions used colour in this way, sometimes deliberately exaggerating the elusiveness and vagueness of colour. Rachel Rooney provides an angry and amusing rant at colour in a poem entitled *Nothing*:

[...]
Yellow's hell. Avoid it.
Yellowness is madness.
Yellow. Break it down and it's the sound it makes.
Yellow. I won't enter it.

Greenness; it isn't me.
Green is somebody else's smell and
green's their home, fingers, mould.
Green grows. Best keep away from it.
[...] (id.: 9)

Its abstract nature might be the reason why colour is often used metaphorically to describe yourself, your body, your skin colour, or someone else's body. Lines such as these from Alison Chisholm's aptly titled poem "Self Colour" not only give colour a very real, fleshy physicality, they might also reflect notions in art and painting to portray a human being as naturalistically as possible:

I am the palette where colour begins:
livid with lung and kidney, liver, heart.

I course with scarlet, draw it back
through indigo veins. Pale cream skin
envelops white of bone, maroons and browns,
brain's grey.
[…] (id.: 11)

I had expected numerous submissions that dealt with the colour of skin, and this was indeed the case, including a moving short story by Tania Hershman, in which a very young child observes his mother's bruises: "He watches her face and sees the dark patch around one eye shift into purple then green then pink. Then there is a new patch, on the other side of her face, below the eye, and that changes colours too." (id.: 67)

An extension of this is the colour of clothes and fabrics, what you chose to cover your body with. This is expressed in two extracts from longer prose pieces, Nisha Woolfstein's "The Impurity of Glass", and Megan Hadgraft's "The Colour Theorists". It was the recurring theme of colour being part of the human body, our physical make-up, which led me to use these lines from Alice Meynell *The Colour of Life* (1896) as the quote that would precede the anthology: "The true colour of life is the colour of the body, the colour of the covered red, the implicit and not explicit red of the living heart and the pulses.
It is the modest colour of the unpublished blood." (id.: 5)

From here, it is only a short leap to deliberately un-naturalistic use of colour in both art and poetry, which was perhaps most fervently executed by the Expressionist movement in both poetry and painting. In early twentieth century expressionist art colour is often used in the form of pure primaries and secondaries, jarring and contrasting for maximum impact, and frequently combined with synaesthesia as a poetic device. I was keen to include an historic example of this use of colour and commissioned Aprilia Zank to translate a poem called *"Der Schlaf"* by Georg Trakl from German into English. Here, Trakl paints an expressionistic picture with words, in a style that resembles that of contemporary painters:

[...]
Dornen umschweben
Den blauen Pfad ins Dorf,
Ein purpurnes Lachen
Den Lauscher in leerer Schenke.
Über die Diele
Tanzt mondesweiß
Des Bösen gewaltiger Schatten
[...]
Thorns hovering
Above the blue path to the village,
A scarlet laughter
The lurker in the empty dive.
Over the floorboard
Dances moonwhite
The Evil's awesome shadow
[...] (id.: 51-52)

Howard Wright's poem "It Would Be", which I placed in first position in the anthology, appeared to me to be a contemporary take on this expressionistic and symbolic use of colour. His poem is at once highly personal and universal, the effect of combining – in a very painterly fashion - the abstract quality of colour with other great, looming abstracts, such as love, memory and language:

If air had a colour it would be green –
those interior shadows, the overhang
and crouching undercut banks; the heat
on the damp and grasping nettles.
If moon had weight it would be gold,
a sovereign moon on the rise,
spending itself on the motorway's roar
and a plane descending the poignant grey.

If language had a sign it would be red,
warning me what not to say
or to tell the truth differently
so it doesn't sound like a lie.

If river had metal it would be silver
and all that is childhood, its surfaces
and forms, memory's torture and time's
hygiene, the slow eddies and depths.
If love had wisdom it would be blue
and irreplaceable, and we would walk
to the viaduct and learn to be alone
because there is no wisdom in love.
(id.: 8)

I received a number of submissions where artists and poets had collaborated on the theme of colour, such as Aprilia Zank and Steve Garside, and Kay Syrad and Gina Glover. In these cases, I was surprised by quite how fluid the collaborative process had been, with the artist and writer often swapping roles. There is clearly scope for a separate publication on this theme. For good measure I also included reactions to art, with the aim of giving non-creative writers a voice. Here is an example by an architect who owns a number of paintings by the recently deceased abstract artist John Hoyland:

In recent paintings, the void, near the centre, occupies
an infin-ity into which one can dive, discover the
beauty of emptiness, and float. Then the eye can settle,
as a butterfly might, upon a flying fragment within the
painting – a glorious moment to feast on blue, orange
and yellow, or red, white, black and yellow. (id.: 55)

Or some of my favourite lines in the anthology, by a curator of photography, Kevin Bacon, on the use of blue in early photography: "But what blue light gave, it also took away. [...] The sea and sky often become reduced to a pale, slightly eerie emptiness." (id.: 30) There is a great immediacy and sometimes accidental poetic beauty in these comments.

I would like to finish this essayistic review of colour, poetry and art by focusing on a recurring theme in the submissions that took me quite by surprise. A large number of the works submitted paired the theme of colour with flowers, specifically roses. There is, of course, a long tradition of flower painting in art, as well as a complex symbolic 'language of flowers'. Interestingly, flower shapes were frequently used by eighteenth and nineteenth century colour theorists and in painting manuals to visualise systems of colour, with the most intriguing example being the colour circle created by Goethe and Schiller in 1799, entitled *Temperament Rose*. An astonishing number of treatises on colour and colour theory of that period were written by botanists or flower painters. An image of the *Temperament Rose* is reproduced in the anthology, as well as corresponding examples by the English colour theorists George Field and Mary Gartside.

In the poems submitted, flowers are featured in various ways. In Catherine Smith's "Xanthophobia", celandines are rampant and a source of dread; Antony Johae's white rose is that of the anti-Nazi group of students who were executed in Munich in 1941, heightened by ideas of purity, freedom and death, whereas Robert Hamberger's "Yellow Roses" uses a literal rose bush as a symbol and metaphor for a lost love, at once memory and sign of renewal:

> When I trickled the dregs of your ashes –
> a teaspoonful washed by spring water –
> on the roots of our wintering roses
> they hit spiky twigs, a clipped waist-high cluster.
> The first time they bloomed I barely noticed.
> I was getting through, too blunted and stunned

to register roses. This year I'm faced
with thirty showy blossoms full as a hand
whose tilted feathers edge every petal,
sunning such glows for as brief as they flower
tickled by bees. A tent of yellow roses tall
as you, hassled with air, a fire tower
calling this summer's drag to crash and burn
while I press my thumb hard against a thorn.
(id.: 43)

In the anthology I placed these very different pieces close together, wondering why colour and flowers are so often used together in art and poetry. Perhaps flowers are perceived as the purest, or at least most visible, manifestation of colour in the natural world, with the added dramatic notion of ephemeral beauty, thus serving certain universal themes that are often the subject of poetry and art.

Bibliography:
Loske, Alexandra (Ed.), 2012, *Languages of Colour*, The Frogmore Press, Lewes, UK

SHARON MORRIS

Sharon Morris trained as a visual artist at the Slade School of Fine Art, University College London, where she teaches. She has performed her poetry with moving images at various venues including Post Gallery, L.A. and King's Place, London. Her poetry has appeared in several journals, such as *Poetry Review, Shearsman, Long Poem Magazine,* and anthologies; *A Room to Live In: A Kettle's Yard Anthology,* 2007; *The Forward Book of Poetry,* 2008; *Rome: A Collection of the Poetry of Place,* 2008; *Poetry tREnD: Eine englisch-deutsche Anthologie zeitgenössischer Lyrik,* 2011. Her first collection, *False Spring,* Enitharmon Press, 2007, was shortlisted for the Aldeburgh Jerwood prize for a first collection. In 2009 she received a Hawthornden Fellowship to work on a new collection, *Gospel Oak,* which was published by Enitharmon Press in January 2013.

These poems are taken from a set entitled, 'Songs of the Aveyron and Ariège: after The Song of Songs'. They came into being through an encounter with a work of art, a series of prints by the American artist Judy Chicago based on the biblical 'Song of Songs'. My encounter with the original Hebrew poem took place through various translations that opened up multiple meanings and gave me the central images of my poems. Staying with friends in the valley of the Aveyron and the Pyrenees, southern France, introduced me to Occitan and the politics of dialect and place, and so this set of poems is threaded with another landscape and language, and represents these encounters.

Extract from **'Songs of the Aveyron and the Ariège: after "The Song of Songs"'**

After the Garrison

Occitan is still spoken,

still sung — *chants d'Auvergne,*
with mountain bagpipes, tambourines
and drums;

a legacy of Latin
after the collapse of Rome,
a language
of idealised love, Troubadour songs;

Occitan of resistance to the Inquisition,
speech of the heretic, the Cathars'
escape from matter,

(all forms of procreation —
eggs, cheese and milk) a language of spirit, pinnacled
impossible high
like those mediaeval towns,
Cordes sur le ciel.

'Who is that rising like the morning star,
clear as the moon, bright
as the blazing sun, daunting
as the stars in their courses!'

In the valley where the Aveyron
meets the Bonnette,
St. Antonin Nobel Val,
there is something welcome,
under this mawkish sun-scape of

canoeing, children laughing, white water, pretty bridges,
                                        trees, old mills, stones,
                        geraniums...

some other tongue —
your mother tongue, *Occitan*,
licking clean the floors of your old home
after the military boots
of Occupation.

            On that simple square of grass circling
around the Mediaeval stocks

            a large corned bull, Ankole, from Africa, a tall-
                        necked llama and a pony
                        with a three-day old foal, trembling, graze:
animal smells, the white breath of animals,
                        this cold morning.
                                    Herald the Circus.

'Before day breathes'

'Before day breathes,

> *before the shadows of night*

are gone' mist nurses
the peaks of these slopes,

> keepsake of the mountain cool, under
the overhanging brow of stones
> that hides the *Isard,*
> > (Pyrenean chamois)
> > lizard and occasional snake —

(zigzag pattern of the *vipère aspic,*
as it scissors its graze over the burning path)

> > bang your stick and
> > stamp your feet!

> > > *'Before day breathes,*
> *before the shadows of night are gone,*
> > *I will hurry to the mountain*
> > > *of myrrh, the hill of frankincense.'*

The GR10, that highway of paths
linking ocean to sea, climbs
> from the valley floor of the Oriège,
> > to a ridge, where a waterfall
> > > is disgorged
into an infinitely blue lake...
> > > *'Oh come with me,*
my bride,
come down with me
from Lebanon. Look down from the peak of Amana...'

The hawk clustered into the blue,

powder-blue sky, keels acrobatic....
       and above, the great raptor, *Aigle royal*, soars
on the wing, for hours, silent
between the fast cross-
path of high-altitude cloud,
scudding into the heaving dark
of the mountain,   and as if
         suicidal

             sky-dives its prey....

        'Look down from Senir
  and Hermon,
from the mountains of the leopards,
        the lions' dens.'

A man suspended under a yellow kite, swings
out from the land on
an armature of sky (honeyed flight
held by hot air)
        his arms sprawled wide

above the tunnel of Paymorens
        to Barcelona,
cut into the jagged cuff
of rock, gouged by glaciers, scarred

by that hammer and pick-axe, that is
        ice, snow, frost,
an arena
that is the breakdown of land and sky,

the march of the sun,
        a scooped hand that is heat —

its bare labour, the Carlit Massif
        of Spain   sun-lit.

Autumn fruits

Purple dying our fingers blue,
                    les mûres mûres,
          our mouths stained
          dark with juice,
                    sweet, tart,

seeds stuck like grit between our teeth —
                    ripe blackberries
on our breath
          pour la confiture
                    and little tarts,

blue-purple taking over
          the white flesh of apple;
                    how love overtakes and
                    the body is taken....

'Your branches are an orchard,
                    Paradise',
(from the Persian, *pardes* —
          P for *peshat*, the literal mind
          R for *remez*, allusion, metonymy,
          D for *derash*, metaphor, symbol,
          S for *sod*, secret)

                    'Your branches
are an orchard of pomegranate trees heavy
          with fruit,
                    flowering henna and spikenard...'

                    Seeds, like white feathers
in a slow glacial drift
to ground —
everything we believed   is abjured.

(published in *Long Poem Magazine*, no. 2, summer 2009)

GRAHAM MUMMERY

Graham Mummery lives in Sevenoaks, Kent. For a time he worked in investment banking and is now training to become a psychotherapist. His poems have appeared in various UK magazines. He is currently working towards his first full collection. Other publications his poems have appeared in include *Gobby Deegan's Riposte* (Donut Press) as well as on websites such as *poetrypf.co.uk*. His own pamphlet, *The Gods Have Become Diseases,* appeared in 2006.

He also has translated poems from French (by René Char, Yves Bonnefoy and Paul Eluard), from German (Goethe and Rilke) and Norwegian (André Bjerke). Some of these have also appeared in magazines and the anthologies of translations from French and German *Over the Water* (Hearing Eye Press, 2007) and *Across Frontiers* (Create Space, 2013). He collaborated in translating from Romanian into English *Deepening the Mystery (EdituraSemene)* by Christiana Maria Purdescu. His own poems have been translated into Romanian and broadcast on *Radio Romania Culture* as part of the *poetry pRO* project, others into German as part of the sister project *poetry tREnD*. He was one of the British poets who attended the W-Orte Festival at Ludwig-Maximillian University, Munich in 2010.

Graham's first full collection of poems is due to be published at the end of 2014 from Pindrop Press.

In my teens, when I read Homer and Goethe for the first time, I came to the conclusion that poetry speaks directly from the deepest levels of our being. I still believe that. Later I found additional models in English, including Blake, Yeats, Ted Hughes and Robert Bly. My reading expanded into other traditions. One of the strongest affinities I feel is with Central and Eastern European poets such as Miroslav Holub and Zbigniew Herbert, as well as those I have attempted to translate for myself. They have all transformed and taught me to express what I have found in my imagination and the external world.

Poem from a Title of Zbigniew Herbert

I would like to describe
the centre of myself
I would like to describe the navel
the omphalos
set where two eagles cross
sent in different directions
by a god seeking
the centre of his world

I would like to describe a place
from which sacred springs
start a river
into a gulf
where tankers pass

to put it another way
these are my veins and arteries
that feed
Islets of Langerhans
the aorta
the corpus callosum

I would like to describe whatever else
feeds thoughts and feelings
as they bathe in
sound light scent
on a shore where
the human body floats
while hands cup
purple pebbles

from there
I would send out
my own eagles

(published in *Brittle Star*, Spring 2011)

On A Summer Night Outside A Pub We Invent A Danish Woman Called David

Não sei quantas almas tenho.
Fernando Pessoa

"Is that possible?" you ask
after our discussion on souls.
But watch how each of us shifts
into her – or is it his? – shape.
Under this lamppost
one struts like Kate Moss on a catwalk,
another affects an Ingrid Bergman accent;
and now you laugh, and ask me
how it feels in this new body.
Tripping in these imaginary high heels,
I'm tempted to ask what other forms
any of us might become this evening:
a gentian, an Evian bottle, a horse.
But, my last train calls. I'll content myself with
the memory of your face, your pink shawl,
and ask which soul drew your laughter lines.

(published in *Ambit 192*, Spring 2008)

The Fallen Wallet

There's the jacket skewered to the chair,
yesterday's socks on the carpet,
the fallen wallet, spine erect:

an open book, innards fanning.
I can lay each page out
reveal a Tarot – the owner's arcanum.

My fingers cross the first card,
its numbers raised – a Nine of Coins
that says its owner is considered

secure for a loan, while
the office pass suggests where he stands
refusing to let the Tower fall.

National Trust, South Bank, R.A.C. –
the Emperor, the Lovers and the Fool –
give other clues, deepen the mystery.

I pull out the licence, see the photo
stare into its eyes – younger, perhaps – ,
match them to my tired face in the mirror.

There's no need
to ask the woman asleep in the bed
if she remembers my name.

(published in *Ambit 198*, Autumn 2009)

Career

I leaped into misty ravines
             landed on a soapy ledge
                         slipped down,
stopped
             held by nylon ropes
                         that I couldn't untie.

Above me, footsteps
             came and went:
                        echoes,
Nietzsche, Jung, Plato,
             Louise Brooks, Doctor Who,
                        who taught me undoing.

"What happened next?"
             I let go,
                        slid into banking,
wrote poems on vouchers.
             Their findings appeared
                        on screens and ledgers.

"And?"
             It paid the bills.
"You've had a career."
             You don't know my career:
                        failed affairs, schemes, utopias.

My failures work better now.
             I'm not the one I thought I was.

(published in *Poetry South East*, 2010)

I Wrestle With A Tiger On The Streets

Down a narrow alley, I scan
paving stones for tiger-prints,
sniff for tiger-droppings,
listen for tiger-roars.

I used to dream of being
a big-game hunter.
When I hear the tiger growl:
"I'd like to wrestle."

Who am I to argue?
He's one big tiger.
We spar. It's quite a scrap.
He tosses me against a wall.

I roll on the ground.
My shoe lands on a paw.
The tiger yelps in pain,
I'm a little winded.

He skids off.
When I wanted to be
the hunter I'd have gone
after him Winchester loaded.

But now I'm a conservationist.
Tigers are rare in these parts.
I stand, wait
watch where he went.

(published in *Brittle Star*, Spring 2011)

PETER PHILLIPS

My life in poetry began in 1994. Five collections have been published; three with *Hearing Eye, No School Tie*, with *Ward Wood Publishing* in 2011, followed by *Oscar and I: Confessions of a Minor Poet* in Spring 2013, also from *Ward Wood Publishing*. In between writing poems, I have co-written two short plays, with Ian Purser, set in the world of writing: 'Stressed Ending' and 'The Green Room'. This has enabled me to enjoy working jointly with another writer and has brought a different dimension to my work.

My writing has enabled me to explore a number of issues and themes common to writers and, more particularly, poets. The latest collection, *Oscar and I: Confessions of a Minor Poet*, departs from my usual voice and introduces the fictional poet, George Meadows. The poems chronicle George's ups and downs as he blunders through his sometimes sad, amusing and eccentric life, where marriage, romance and friendship collide with poetry, his beloved dog Oscar and his love of wine. Poems have been published in leading literary magazines and I often give readings.

I especially enjoy meeting other writers and like participating in events here and abroad, which are so important in fostering a common understanding of other cultures and literary traditions. These poems have been carved mainly from life experience. They are typical of the subjects that engage me, being a mix of experience, imagination and that other elusive ingredient – poetic truth – where another dimension, however small and at first, seemingly insignificant, can make a difference. This can be represented by language and form, but very often emotion and feeling. A poem will be inspired by a memory or image. It's when these are at their strongest that I know I've got to write the poem.

Bath Time Butterflies at Boarding School

A butterfly comes to rest,
level with my eyes, on the edge of the bath.

She's a Painted Lady – I'd been praying
to see one soon – and her wings quiver

in the steamy heat of the water.
She flits to my stomach, settles between

my thighs. Then others fly in,
Red Admirals, Large Whites, more Painted Ladies,

a mass of wings fanning the glow
in a swirl of colour, till their flutter

giddies me in a breathless rainbow rush
and they're flying to another fourteen-year-old.

It was better than scoring a penalty,
even Mother sending money.

I tell myself I'll give up the butterflies
when I've seen them ten times,

but after I get to double figures, I lose count.

(published in *No School Tie*, Ward Wood Publishing, 2011)

The Acer Tree

We saw it learn to dance
then pirouette and arabesque
bloom into leaf as it grew,

thirty years from a wisp of air
into a ballerina, branches
picking up light and grace in the breeze.

Now it sways in the garden,
rhythmically shading the lawn,
reminding me of you.

(published in *No School Tie*, Ward Wood Publishing, 2011)

Roast Potatoes

Roast potatoes have their eccentricities
and like a friend or lover
I don't like them perfect,
too fluffy, too mumsy in the middle,

I like my potatoes a little burnt,
a crisp crunch in the mouth.
I don't mind a chase round the plate,
some foreplay – but just a bit.

A heap of roast potatoes
is a kiss on the neck,
a frog, all heartbeat, sitting on a water lily leaf –
so much better than a pile of peas.

I like them on a Friday night
in my mouth, in my lap, in my hands,
I just love roast potatoes
any way at all.

(published in *Wide Skies, Salt and Best Bitter*, Hearing Eye, 2005)

The Poetry Critic

I'm George Meadows. You weren't very generous
about my last book. In fact you verged
on the rude. Didn't you understand the poems?

Oh, there was something to understand, was there?

There you go again. Were you born rude
or is it an affectation?

I don't have to stand here and listen to this.

Where would you rather go then?

I'll see you're never reviewed again.

I suppose you're just one of those people
who can't do it, so they review it.
Wasn't there anything you liked about my work.

Actually, I was rather taken with the way you write
about wine, use the grape as a metaphor for love
and passion. Like me, you know your wine.

Yes, this is true, I do like what I like. You wouldn't care
to share a bottle, would you?

I thought we were enemies.

Oh I don't think so. That's all forgotten,
especially since you'll be buying.

(published in *Oscar and I*, Ward Wood Publishing, 2013)

Forest Fox

He sensed my hesitation, untangled
my thoughts, disappeared before the sound
of heartbeat crossed the clearing.
Why do foxes think they're God's gift?

I followed, felt the ground give, squelch
of boots in mud and moss, heard the crack
of twigs as I plodded after him. He scampered
away, called me on, barked my name.

The rain came so cold it scorched
my cheeks and still the fox howled onwards,
turned his head towards me as he fox-trotted
through the fist of the forest.

On till gloom became darkness. We stopped.
He faced me. His drowned eyes stared
as he nosed the air; his coat was frost,
his mouth spit and steam.

I crouched to within a sniff of his face,
dared to ask, 'Do you believe...
and who will remember you when you die?'
'It's not about belief,' he said.

I reached and touched his head, felt slicked down
crisp fur, saw that fox as I would never
again; then he licked me, turned, bounded off,
faded into the thick of morning mist.

(published in *Looking For You*, Hearing Eye, 2001)

Love

Most think it will last for ever,
others wait for it to end.
A few decide it will never happen,
many hope and some pretend.

(published in *Wide Skies, Salt and Best Bitter*, Hearing Eye, 2005)

ALAN PRICE

Alan Price is a London poet who has been a guest poet at Torriano Poets and read widely on the poetry circuit. He organises *Poets off the Shelf* (a bi-monthly poetry event) held in Camden. Alan has been published in such magazines as *Envoi, Orbis, Poetry Monthly, The Interpreter's House, Essence, Obsessed with Pipework, The Morning Star Newspaper, The Delinquent, The Royal Shakespeare Company* website (and other online e – magazines). Poems were featured in Aoife Mannix's anthology *Postcards from Leather Lane* (2010), the Ruth O'Callaghan poetry anthologies *Genius Floored* (2009), *Seeking Refuge* (2010), *A Shadow on the Wall* (2011) and *Alphabet of Days (2012)*. In 2010, his poem 'Festive End' was a runner up in the Camden Libraries History Poem competition.

Apart from writing poetry, Alan is also a scriptwriter and has written four short films directed by Pawel Regdosz. The trailer for their latest film *Pack of Pain* can be viewed online at IMDB. The film has won four international film festival awards. Alan's TV film *A Box of Swan* (starring Pete Postlewhaite) was screened on BBC 2 (1990) and subsequently published. Alan's short story / novella collection *The Other Side of the Mirror* (an alternative take on the vampire myth) came out in 1999 from Citron Press. Other stories have also been broadcast on BBC Radio 3 and published in paperback anthologies. Alan returned to writing poetry five years ago, after a gap of twenty years. Although fiction and screen writing have their challenges, he feels that it is in poetry that his most authentic writing voice can be best expressed. Alan's debut collection of poetry *Outfoxing Hyenas* was published by Indigo Dreams Publishing in October 2012.

Poetry, like music and film, draws upon many sources for its inspiration. Today there is an even greater number of people writing poetry of differing content and styles. Poetry is still, as Yeats said, 'The dialogue with your self.' However, I believe that such a dialogue should not stay private. It also needs to jump onto the stage, overlap, or listen into, the self dialogues that other poets, at home and abroad, are conducting. Poets should accept that such encounters might just unravel our assumed certainties about what constitutes a poem, and hopefully make our writing more explorative and, thus, better.

For Forty Seven Read Twenty Nine
(for Luigi Pirandello)

At the hotel lobby my key forty seven
was obstinately kept on hook twenty nine.
Right you are, if you think so, Mr. Pirandello.
The manager smiled at my joke.

In Agrigento lie the headquarters of Kaos
where Luigi was born silver spoon in mouth,
tasting of sugar, codes of honour and Sicilian doubt.
Tonight there's a full moon.
You can see the steep gorge below the house,
recently blackened by an arbitrary fire,
and smell the childhood scent
of his beloved pine.
I stand with a pocket torch at the gate.
Taxi waiting for my return.
A madman likely to be arrested.

For forty seven read twenty nine.
What does it matter?
Illusory key. Illusory room. Illusory hotel.
Perhaps only a presence passed through.
Wavered over the wrong key hook.
Was allowed respite
from the great not knowing.

(published in *Finger Dance Festival* Website, 2009)

Heron Land

Another age wore the plumage of herons.
Fashionable ladies no longer adorned.
Wetlands destroyed. Plume trade died.
Herons protected – eighteen eighty nine.
Royal Society guarding all its egrets.

Here residents, without wings, born too late
for conservation. Scraped dry of worldly
marsh. Bred to wait in the drying lounge.
Stone heron, on the home's gate, generating
no sign of morning, only a last signal for night.

Abandoned of stick, frame, back of chair.
'I can't. I won't. I need more air.'
Squeezed between incontinent cream
bed sores on spine promote the wailing.
Care assistant, chewing gum, keeps on trailing
all the day's excreta, too noisy to dream.
The noise wiped clean, one leg made neat.
'Where am I? What's for dinner? Is it cold meat?'

Swift he measures, smoothes down the wall.
Once a profitable, perfect plasterer.
No tools now, no motion to master.
The mind, in his gaps, starting to crack.
Sealed. Invisible. Like the job gaping back.

'Ash on trousers. Why am I stained?
I'll piss them clean. Who needs their aid?
They piss you about…a dictatorship.
I can't sit here biting my lip.
I'm not an old man. She's not an old dear.
Hang out your prick…there's nothing to fear.
They vacuum your body of such thoughts.

Polish your head till nothing snorts.
Sweets, biscuits, tissues…a drink?
They're buggers but yet I stink
To bugger something far too old,
their fear of me, how I mould.'

She furiously walks as if walking space
finally offered a life she could face.
Up and down stairs, her stretched blue eyes
view what's journeyed without surprise.
Dining room, kitchen, first floor, second.

Walks become her maelstrom errand,
out of which whirls a kiss, a greeting.
'I'm going home. You know whom I'm meeting.'

Swallowed whole the Jonah people sleep.
Drugged in a whale's stomach bleeding.
Valium veiled, too weak to prise the jaws.
Quizzical they dream. Re-counting their years.
'I'm almost a hundred…is that why I'm tired?'

Matron, removing dark glasses, points hard
at ancient mouths. Here primal sounds are pasted.
'Before / Then / I was / I used to'
That claw of talking in past tense
makes gaunt grammar instilling dense
the lie that you've backward gone
and personality's over & done.

Reluctant visitors turn up, out of fear.
'Look at the lines of this thing's face.'
Its broken contours they'll markedly share.
Differently marked, equally hated.
Broken or brittle in their leftovers.

Begging memories, of Mother, to return
and shield of this encroaching place.

We started of wrong, were given the fright.
Great ageing. That's a disease, queer beings catch.
Atomised. Diagnosed. Quarantined
from a young vampirish economy.
Bundled asleep for the social inventory.
Standing coldly communal or solitary.
Old herons divided against themselves.
Streams, empty of fish, were no one delves.

Pas De Deux

The devil came to me last night.
Violently argue with that waitress in her sunken bar?
Later, she and I drank beer over vodkas of fire.

The devil came to me this morning.
A small black impish glowing thing.
Its wings beating against my beating head.

It bared its teeth, stuck out its ears, wiggled
a pair of horns shaped like sore red gums.
Assumed the body of a midget ballerina.

Fonteyn, with fangs, danced on my bed.
Then flew round the room like a moth, on heat,
for an old man's musty clothes, watching me with gritty eyes.

I sat upright and waited. Playing a grating polka,
the satanic figurine attacked with a black accordion.
My arms and legs began to twitch in horror.

It danced me round the room. Up the walls and ceiling.
Like a woken bat I obeyed its pulling out of the stops.
Music to drug and damn all my helpless senses.

I crashed to the floor with diabolic partner.
This imp crawled up my naked leg. Halted at the knee cap.
Pirouetted on the bone. Accordion playing solo on my chest.

Polka scrapped. Now a nutcracker began to advance.
As the morning light grew brighter, I shut down my eyes.
Pas De Deux croaked the thing. *Pas De Deux!*

ANNA ROBINSON

Anna Robinson was born and lives in London. She has an MA in Public History from Ruskin College, Oxford. Her pamphlet, *Songs from the flats* (Hearing Eye 2006), was a Poetry Book Society Pamphlet Choice. In 2001, she became the first recipient of The Poetry School Scholarship and her poetry was featured in the School's second anthology, *Entering the Tapestry,* (Enitharmon 2003). Her work has appeared in several journals and anthologies, including *Poetry London, Magma, Brittle Star, the reater, In The Company of Poets* (Hearing Eye 2003) and *Oxford Poets 2007* (Oxford/Carcanet). A former tutor in prisons, she is a regular poetry judge for the Koestler Competition and is a founding editor for *Not Shut Up!* and the newly established *Long Poem Magazine.* Her first poetry collection *The Finders of London,* Enitharmon Press, 2010, was shortlisted for the inaugural Seamus Heaney Poetry Centre Prize for Poetry in 2011.

I think all poetry writing is an act of translation. You are using the language of the conscious mind to say something that is coming from the subconscious.

I ran a project where I collected 'old phrases' that were largely euphemisms. Then I got other people from the same community to define them. Some differences of definition were explainable on the basis of the personality of the definer. However, some differences of interpretation were broader than that, and it made me wonder if we ever really understand what each other is saying. Poetry, to me, rises to meet that challenge. Sometimes people say "some things are beyond words!" No poet should ever say this. To say this is to give up before you have started. Poetry is about saying that which is beyond words – in words!

Agnus

Lamb, I have seen you from trains.
I have seen you as I walked through fields.
You looked back at me, raised
your left hoof towards me in a delicate way.
Lamb, I have found your winter curls
by the roadside, on thorns and on barbed wire.

Lamb, who exalts what the world gets wrong
its failings, its struggles, honourable lamb
feel for us.

Lamb, all winter I wear black to absorb the sun.
Red is not as good at this. It is only for inside.
Lamb, my mother had a dream.
The whole family lived separately in sheds
in the back yard. It was dark and cold.
When we went to find each other, we weren't there.

Lamb, who exalts what the world gets wrong
heals wounds, smooths troubles, loving lamb
feel for us.

Lamb, these derelict testaments are stained.
They're cased in walls of clay. We cannot reach them.
We are damp and raucous, our marsh overgrown.
The trees under our pavements are dead. The stairs,
by which you left to sail up river, lead nowhere.
Lamb, why do we fear ourselves?

Lamb, who exalts what the world gets wrong
crowns hags, creates doubt, fragrant lamb
give us peace.

(published in *Brittle Star, Spring 2011*)

Show Pansies

The blooms should be thick and circular,
no waviness in the petals, they should
possess a glossy, velvet appearance.
In Kill 'em and eat 'em Street, we watch.

The face of the bloom should be slightly
arched or convex, with a small eye.
The dustbin lids have gone missing again.

The two centre petals should meet above
and reach well up on the top two.
The landladies are on the roof.

The lower petal should be sufficiently
deep and broad for balance and each
should lie evenly upon the others.
They can't find them either.

To elaborate further, the top of the lower
petal should be straight and flat.
But look what they've spotted.

The two centre petals should be arranged
evenly on either side of an imaginary
line drawn through the yellow eye.
Someone's hanging out washing at number 3.

The top of these petals should reach to the same
height on the upper petals so that the whole
of the bloom is evenly balanced.
It isn't Monday. Someone will pay.

(published in *Reactions*, 4, 2003 and in *Songs from the Flats*, 2005,
Hearing Eye)

Ghosting

I wake where I was sleeping
in my room
but the walls are gone
and all I see are night shapes
twisting away from the bed.
They're brambles, I think,
yes, they are, and in full fruit
and now I can feel the night's a warm one
and now I can feel there is no breeze.

Trying to find my bearings
by the moon
and the brown-mirrored rear
of the department of health
always to its right
which has gone, like the fence
to the park, like the park and the flats
and now I can see the shapes of out-houses
and now I can see the moon on glass.

I get up and not finding
my slippers,
walk on through grass,
which in part is boggy
which is not such a bad thing
and as it's a full moon
I see the flowers, folded for sleep,
Viola tricolor, tickle me fancy,
heartsease, jump up and kiss me.

(published in *Reactions*, 4, 2003 and in *Songs from the Flats*, 2005,
Hearing Eye)

Renovations

It's foolish to think there'd be no conflict
the scaffold closes in on us, blocks

the light-stream and it doesn't rain.
Our pansies are dead. They will not regenerate.

The cold new doors come: too fast, too heavy
and we're stuck behind them, eye to little eye,

stomach driven, planning our resistance;
but the new windows will not break

and we've forgotten how to destroy steel.
The landladies talk of how nice it will be

how much we'll like it when it's done.
On Fridays we blow their dust off our tools

I rub my saw, my iron mallet,
my neighbour shines up his hammer.

The empty baskets and window boxes avoid
our eyes. Yes, we're waiting, we are waiting.

(published in *Songs from the Flats*, 2005, Hearing Eye)

Pansy Neilson's Magnificent

This is not the leper house,
it's not here that lesions creep
through a bright red haze.

That's on the other side -
where they've put builders' huts
over the football pitch.

What is this haze - smudging out
from the blotch to form a margin?
It's red as in heart not iron

or blood, a red too Victorian
to stand for this place,
too red for the likes of us.

(published in *Reactions*, 4, 2003 and in *Songs from the Flats*, 2005,
Hearing Eye)

JULIE-ANN ROWELL

Julie-ann Rowell's pamphlet collection *Convergence* was selected as a recommended read by the Poetry Book Society. Her first full collection, *Letters North,* was nominated for the Inaugural Michael Murphy Memorial Award for Best First Collection in Britain and Ireland, 2011. She teaches poetry in Bristol and serves on the ExCite committee for the enhancement of poetry in Devon.

Our gathering in London was a stimulating meeting of minds and cultural exchange. Poetry needs this kind of interaction in order to stay vivid and authentic. The conversations that took place and the readings of individual poems fired my imagination for a long time afterwards. It was a pleasure to encounter such diversity and vibrancy, such colour and enthusiasm. May such collaborations long continue!

Invitation

In her letters she talks mostly of her garden,
while I listen for the invitation,
imagine the snow's retreat, soft round hills,
the pink haze of Oslo early morning.

While I listen for the invitation
she writes of hard earth and change,
the pink haze of Oslo early morning,
how she likes to greet a stranger.

She writes of hard earth and change
as if I've never experienced such things,
how she likes to greet a stranger,
I try to remember her smile, her grace,

as if I've never experienced such things
the longer days and warmer nights.
I try to remember her smile, her grace,
dream of arriving, and how that might be.

The longer days and warmer nights
reflected here, but I feel cold,
dream of arriving and how that might be,
of the fullness of spring and its joy

reflected here, but I feel cold.
She writes long letters, but less and less
of the fullness of spring and its joy,
nothing else rises to the surface.

She writes long letters, but less and less,
while I listen for her invitation –
nothing else rises to the surface.
Oslo is somewhere I visited once long ago.

While I listen for her invitation
she notes the love of her children, husband.
Oslo is somewhere I visited once long ago
all fading into fragments, jaded.

She notes the love of her children, husband.
I turn the page and turn the page, memories
all fading into fragments, jaded.
In her letters she talks mostly of her garden.

('Invitation' was chosen as one of the top 25 poems in the Mslexia Women's Poetry Competition, 2010, and published in *Mslexia* magazine, issue 47.)

Jerusalem

Under silent fig trees, the sky's a too solid blue
like a picture in a children's bible.

The guide leads in a patina of shade, always thinking
of their comfort, he has the softest tread

of anyone she's met. It is a land filled
with honey and vines, he says. She notices

a pomegranate tree in a courtyard, and the call to prayer in the
morning, as he pulls them

further in with his orchestrated words; his eyes
find her when she looks up.

At the Wailing Wall they stand clear
of the devotions, an English hymn

that she cannot place, and Sundays avoiding
church, strolling through lacy grass to home,

and the Jerusalem Cherry that wasn't anything to do
with Jerusalem though it drew the picture –

the berries deadly apparently, though later this
was contradicted, like so many things.

He is gently herding them again, down
claustrophobic streets to the next temple, the next shrine;

she's avoided God all these years. The guide
says Jerusalem is the most Holy city.

She craves that little courtyard and the sun
even more ancient here, turning circles for God.

('Jerusalem' was Shortlisted for the Wells Poetry Prize, 2011)

The Lower Ninth Ward

They called it the drowning, the progress
of water against the windows. She said she saw

a mongrel struggle to climb onto a table,
as if it were a surfboard, front legs splayed,

and called to him in vain. The world's
possessions sailed by, including the dog.

Curious what floated, she never would have
guessed – even the neighbour's truck.

Finally, she climbed onto the roof.
The wind had eaten part of it exposing

the skeleton of her house, and there
she stayed with the pet rabbit out of its cage

the warm pulse of its body giving her hope,
but no one came for days. The air was rank:

what muck had been stirred up, what exposed?
Like everything, it was all mixed in.

The world had left with the water. Now just
the lap of darkness, her camera recording.

Regent's Park

He often mentioned how his father took him
at the close of day, to the park, and they
held still in the beginning of dark,
as the Manitoba wolves began their call.

The animals couldn't be seen beyond
the wire fence only the howling
of those long maned souls, and the boy
dreamed of them in the snow peaks

of Canada, running so fast they blurred.
Here in the city, it was like a secret between
only them, how the wolves communicated
as if their space ran for thousands of miles

of nothing but scrub and dirt, and wind
in their faces. The boy imagined
shapes in the blackness, argent livery,
with no need for reason, except just for being.

Now, finding the park unchanged,
the elaborate gates, the electric fences,
he wants to pitch howl for his father
the cry of the wild just the same.

The Lantern Maker

Mr Lu's workshop is crammed with dragons, lions,
unicorns, frogs, fish, lobsters, rabbits, lotus blossoms
of silk and paper, cut and pasted by hand in the pressing
heat, singular cold, from the time of the first Ming emperor.
The little paper water-lilies designed to be floated on water,
are minutely and evenly scored, folded and crimped
into the night by the silent fingers of Mr Lu and Mr Lu's wife.

There is no one else to carry through his magnum opus –
a nine-dragon set-piece in red, green, blue and yellow.
'Nowadays young folk can't stick at it for even a day,' says
Mr Lu, seventy and working still, in spite of Mao.
 'Colour and form', he says, 'is what it's all about.'
Mr Lu's workshop is crammed with lotus blossoms, rabbits,
lobsters, fish, frogs, unicorns, lions and dragons.

ANNE STEWART

Apart from writing terrible songs and scribbling some (occasionally not bad) verse, Anne Stewart led a virtually poetry-free – more significantly, poetry-ignorant – life until, in 1993, Wendy Cope's *Serious Concerns* was brought to her attention. Suddenly, many things were clear. Since then, her love of poetry has been unshakeable and she has changed her life-style to make poetry her own serious concern. She was awarded an MA (Dist) in Creative Writing from Sheffield Hallam University, where she studied with Sean O'Brien and, in 2008, won the Bridport Prize. Her first collection, *The Janus Hour*, was published by Oversteps Books in 2010. She founded *poetry p f*, a web-based showcase of poets, from which arose the two translation collaborations, *poetry pRO* (English/Romanian with Lidia Vianu, University of Bucharest) and *poetry tREnD* (English/German with Aprilia Zank, Ludwig-Maximilian University, Munich), and she is Administrator for Second Light, a network of women poets.

I'm constantly amazed at how poetry can communicate the most complex of concepts and emotions. Poetry is the only art form that does this for me. I'm impressed by its ability to cross a cultural divide, giving unexpected insights into another way of thinking; challenging the inherent 'rightness' of our own mind-set. Realising the linguistic encounter with virtual and actual meetings with other poets and translators is a bonus – a nice shiny gift tied up in ribbons of scarlet and gold... and if it should turn out that I contribute a poem or two to the canon... well, I'd consider that a real achievement.

A bed is a light bulb in the night sky

See how it tugs itself off and on off and on.
See it suck in the stars swelling its brightness
exhale them in uneven spatters of light in the sky.

A bed is a light bulb that tugs you to half-sleep
disjointedly dreaming impossible circles
impossible circles in search of solutions

that tugs you to half-wake afraid of the night
of impossible circles stalking the morning
the light at the crack of the creak of a door.

A bed is a light bulb lit by a mind of its own.
See how it clings to the night sky above you
too high to permit you to harry it down.

See it as scowler growling and clawing its litter
of clouds. See how it prowls in impossible circles
settles its score for you tethering it to the ground.

A bed is a light bulb in the night sky vengeful
determined. You must sew up your eyes know
that the meter must run out of shillings sometime.

(published in *ARTEMISpoetry*, Issue 9, November 2012)

Feathers

'Unable to establish the date and time'
was what distressed me – if he was mine,
if he was my father, I'd want to know
the when and how the going was,
hoping not too turbulent or tough
for such an independent man –

so I focus on that gorgeous photograph
of him with the birds in St James's park,
their fast wings flapping, wafting his hair
as though he was braving a minor gale,
feathers everywhere, and all his malice
gone out of him to who knows where.

I want it to have been only the night before
(*Heard from dad? There's been no card or call*)
and that the brother called because he knew,
not just suspected. I want it to be that mystical
event I know can occur in spite of distances
and what's not known: that he 'felt him go'.

The night my grandfather died, I woke up
bolt upright in bed and cried, distressed
for who knew why – I'd had no nightmare,
I recall no visitation, no semblance of goodbye.
Holding out my palm, I purse my lips,
blow gently, watch the feathers rise.

(published in *ARTEMISpoetry*, Issue 7, May 2011)

What the Beast Didn't Know

Cinderella was her sister – identical twins and mutual devotees.
That sweaty slipper was a set-up. He never knew,
the prince, that it was Beauty's shoe.

In the pocket of her pinafore, there were three beans,
already plump and ready to pass the genome on,
courtesy of a simpleton.

One summer, fallen on hard times, all through the long
hot nights, she'd been a lap-dancer in Jamahallabaad.
No regrets. No need for an Iliad.

Nor did she mind a barrel or two of gold and oil.
Talk her way through rock, she could.
Make any old lamp come good.

She knew all about apples, spells and dragons,
hedges of thorns. How to make a lover kill and kiss,
steal the maiden and the myth.

And love? The father and the rose, a prince at last?
She wrote the book – trimmed the tales beyond the chapter
that promises happily ever after.

(published in *Ariadne's Thread*, Issue 2, Summer 2012)

Perception as a Furry Thing

Why must men sit so suggestively on trains?
This one is big and heavy. Aging new man,
a campaign of clean, oozing the cleverness of gym.
Legs wide apart and buttocks hunkered in,
of course, where else to slant his bottle down
but bang-slap-centre close up in between?
I toss about the he-does-he-doesn't-know of it;
appreciate the chunky awkwardness proclaiming,
in ebullient tone, that "It's a comfort thing".

But, then, that's men. "Men come pre-validated"
according to the Stewart Theory of Easy Successful Men
(i.e. the ones who don't spend much time wondering what,
of anything they've ever done, they could do better than).
He stretches toes at me, looks me in the eye and grins,
fingers tightening on the bottle in his lap. I'm thinking
Cheek of him and *Well, no mistake there then*
when I spot the hat. Bang-slap-centre, the black
and softly furry hat I'm always cradling in mine.

(published at *Translation Café* 2009)

Taking the Alice Road

> "When you walk with me, I can feel
> you changing down several gears"
> Alice Beer (age 93)

A Model T is scurrying at snail's pace along the Alice Highway.
Out of a slip road shoots a brand new Ford Capri. It overtakes,
excited by its own idea of destination

but when it sees the Model T, admires her modest choice
of livery, it slows to hear her ancient engine, her wise
puttering in Walter Mitty mode

ta pocketta pocketta cutting through its own souped-up
racing purr. It changes down a gear, and then another,
and another, until the two cars

are keeping company. They cruise sedately. Ta pocketta prrr,
ta pocketta prrr. The Alice Highway shimmers into infinity.
You can see eternity from here.

(published in anthology *Lyrical Beats*, Rhythm & Muse, 2012)

Grasshopper

The trouble with the perfect tune,
the one your blood will always rise to,
is, it's wispy. The trick is that you
have to sing along. Stop joining in,
even for a moment, it's as good as gone.
Sing all night, given half a chance to.
You know a feisty female still has one
antennae cocked to another's song.

(published in collection *The Janus Hour*, Oversteps Books, 2010)

Piete

When I go out with the junk papers in the dark,
ready for morning, Peter is smoking.
Hello, Pete, how are you doing? I say,
then *Don't you usually smoke in the back?*
and he sends me a half-laugh, making me
remember him, as he came out last Tuesday,
to find me smoking in the front. Six days on
and, with that and less than half a look,
he has me listening to us then:
him *I didn't know you smoked*
and me *Relapses.*

We fall silent to watch the little coughs
of smoke rise from Peter's lips
as he exhales, slow and far.

His life has changed. I have questions.
I want to ask him – everything! –
but I've been reading Platonov,
so I feel Russian and I only ask
Was it a big change, Piete?
and now he's Russian too.
I watch the weight of his words
bruise his throat. *It's better.*
he tells me, with the look of a man
who knows words can't cover it.

We stand silent for a minute,
maybe two, only his smoke
alive in the night, listening
for something. Something small
and much less Russian.

(published in the anthology *Bridport Prize: The Winners 2010*)

GEORGE SZIRTES

George Szirtes was born in Budapest in 1948 and came to England with his family as refugees following the Hungarian Uprising in 1956. Brought up in London, he went to art college for five years, met his wife, painter Clarissa Upchurch, then spent a long time in Hertfordshire and is currently spending a long time in Norfolk. His first book, *The Slant Door* (1979) was joint winner of the *Faber Memorial Prize* and he has written many since then, the most recent being *Reel* (2004) which was awarded the *T S Eliot Prize*, *The Burning of the Books* (2009) and *Bad Machine* (2013) both the latter shortlisted for the T. S. Eliot Prize. In between came a mammoth *New and Collected Poems* (2008), both in e-book form and in the solid flesh of paper. He has been translating poetry and fiction from the Hungarian since 1984, his most recent translation, of László Krasznahorkai's *Satantango*, being awarded the *Best Translated Book Award* 2013 in the USA. His children's book, *In the Land of the Giants,* won the *CLPE Award* 2013 for best book of poetry for children. It has been a rather extraordinary year. He has won other things but that's quite enough about prizes.

Most of his life he has been teaching one thing or another and that, in effect, has been his own education. He has taken somewhat enthusiastically to Twitter and has been writing long sequences of texts for the medium, and has collaborated with poet Carol Watts on an uncharacteristic sequence of fifty-six poems, titled "56". A lover of form under pressure he is always looking for various ways to induce pressure into form

Spleen

After Baudelaire

I'm like the king of a rainy country, rich
but wobbly weak, both cub and toothless bitch.
I'm through with books, and poems and string quartets :
I've sold the horses, shot the household pets.
Cheer up? Not likely, board games are a bore
and as for 'the people' dying by my door,
fuck them, and fuck that guitar-wielding clown,
who's worse than useless when I'm feeling down.
See, here he is – that's me – stuck in his bed,
the girls can put on sex shows, give him head,
go girl on girl, no point, it just won't work,
it won't jump-start this junky royal jerk.
The quack who brings him pills and knows a trick
to harden flaccid aristocratic dick,
may as well bring blood and the Roman Baths,
the kind that suited those old psychopaths.
No good, he's dead in muscle, nerve, and brain.
It's all green Lethe and that bloody rain.

The Night, The Books, The Calm

The dead of night. Time
of day between beginning
and continuing.

There was the bed and there were the books. The body was still
a child. The rain was still one drop after another. It was how
things were.
*

The body was ranged in order. The books were defence and
ordnance. The ordinary days rose and fell.
*

Order was calm. The night was calm. The books kept their
covers closed. There were neither birds nor rain. Only time was
restless, untoward.
*

What stories wanted telling? What was the calm at the heart of
the stories? Where was the clearing in the forest that started the
stories?
*

There we could invent life as if it were a story. There trees spoke
the language of invention. We ordered the trees and language
into life.
*

What we woke into was story. What sleep interrupted was
story. We dreamed the broken stories into order, into breath and
calm.
*

Trees, words, dreams of order. The terms simple, the night
calm, the waking a language arranging itself around a clearing.
*

It was sweet waking and arranging things, sweet folding the
words into woods. As if one could unfold them any time, in any
order.
*

Dead of night. The time
between continuities,
that small padded space.

The Covering

Between two panes of glass the signs of neglect:
a piece of fuzz, lint, or down that trembles in the draught
of the vent, like a tiny unsustainable craft
on an ocean it cannot solve or perfect.

Now that the wind is up everything beyond
is in a frazzle. The clothes on the line, frail
twigs, the clouds, the whole world setting sail
to an unknown continent over a galactic pond.

Mind too hovers. This is the last day of days,
the crackpots declare, as if days were other than last,
as if we could carry on for ever, not hovering.

As for the fuzz, lint, or down, it holds fast
to the glass either side while the draught plays
across it, as if air were sea, the glass a covering.

(published in *Bad Machine*, Bloodaxe, 2013)

Fish Music
For Pascale Petit

He struggles into his borrowed human skin,
the one he wears for special occasions
with the sewn-in dinner jacket and polished patent feet.
He brushes off earth and other traces of night,
Smells the remnant darkness on his sleeve,
Bends back the fingers that constitute his living,
And picks up the instrument. His mother is listening
In the next room, holding her breath for him,
The breath she has been saving all her adult years.

After the skin, the fish scales. One must glitter.
One must swim through the day. He flicks his tail
This way and that. He makes the first sounds
Those scraped sighs that are the sign of his well-being.
'I'm ready,' he says, his eyes glassy and round.
'I've got my gills on. The whole amphibian kit.'

The music begins. The sea waits by the door.
Both skin and scale are glowing. The neck he wears
Is just a little loose, he must tighten it.
The chin has worn away on his left side.
The music slops about inside his belly a while
Then creeps upward blowing through his ears
Into the room and hard against the walls.
Now he is swimming. He sees the music
Floating in the tank of the room. He must practice harder.
It is his food after all. He can feel its strands
Slip between his fingers, now silk, now knife.
It smells wholesome, of water, night and skin.

'How does it sound?' he asks her. 'Like salt,' she says,
'Like salt and damascene.' Her fancy talk, he thinks.

It's not his skin, he knows that. The dinner jacket
Is of another era. Too many buttons on the waistcoat
Of the flesh. Too much blood in the fibre, none of it his.
But music too is skin. He wraps it about him.
He's hardly there: half-fish-half-man is elsewhere,
In the bone beneath a skin that's not his own.
Each living thing has its own element, he thinks,
And even this old skin belongs to someone.

(published in *Bad Machine*, Bloodaxe, 2013)

Easy Listening

It was the long melodic lines that held them together,
chords wound about the limbs of the expected.
When they were falling apart it was what protected
their fragile heads from turning into lather.

They wanted passions they recognised in their sleep
because their sleep had never been unbroken.
There were too many mornings they had woken
to ice, fire, exhaustion, filth; to the cheap

Music others referred to, that they themselves held dear,
their clichés priceless and dark as their own lives:
Songs without Words, Für Elise, the long knives
of aspiration sharpening in the ear.

(published in *Bad Machine*, Bloodaxe, 2013)

ADELE WARD

Adele Ward lives in London with her sons, Stefano and Danny, and her chihuahua Max. She was born in Belfast and moved regularly with her family before settling in London, where she has lived most of her adult life, apart from a four-year spell in Milan, Italy. She is a poet, novelist, journalist and co-owner of *Ward Wood Publishing*.

Poetry is often described as a small world where everybody knows everybody else, and I disagree with that. There are so many good poets who can be off our radar because of the tendency to get together for readings in regions. This has led to poets and poetry readers being familiar with the big national and international names and also the poets most active in their local venues and publications. Luckily this is changing due to the internet and excellent projects like Poets in Person. *I have always studied languages to be able to read original versions of books and enjoy the way the internet lets international poets and poetry readers communicate and work together.* Poets in Person *takes this a step further, with events where we can meet up with poets from around the world face-to-face to share our poems and dialogue.*

I have included poems which have a focus on poetry inspired by art from other cultures, and also one of my love poems to London, my adopted home and a place where many cultures meet in person and in poetry.

Londoner

The Thames is my mother –
cold and dark and powerful
as she should be.
Letting me go until I forget
then find myself, one night,
by the tug of her tide
and know: home.

My father was sheer accident
like a visit from a god,
unneeded after.
She drives her own course.
St Paul's an eccentric uncle in the corner
who had no children of his own.
Fixed in the clothes of his youth
he smiles at great-nieces.

My siblings are these people
jogging by; the tourists,
frustrated businessmen, and newly arrived
who crowd with many languages.
My mother adopts them all
and sees no difference.
She is accepting, alone and loveless –
setting us free. Taking us back.

Stress

(Inspired by the Catherine Yass film High Wire featuring Didier Pasquette)

Some people have a fear of falling upwards
when they raise their eyes to the top of a tower block.
They feel their feet might leave the ground,
as if gravity could release them
to fall through clouds and vanish
just because they look up.
They are afraid to glance.

The high-wire walker knows gravity
from the rooftops, joins high rises
in a dot-to-dot, makes it look easy
as the wind fills his ears like a plane on take-off.

The only way is to slide each footstep forwards
in his own ballet, tasting the blood metallic
rust of the wire, believing it
to be just one metre off the ground, like the one
at home, where he has fallen many times.

The concrete of the blocks tells him
the fall will not be through the clouds,
but down, hard, and ugly,
as the windows spool past, a movie reel fast forward,
with all his admirers watching.

Unconditional

I carried my mother on my back

               -Yayoi Kusama

I carry my mother on my back
in an infant sling, she weighs me down,
always close.
Sometimes she curls around her pain
in the pit of my belly.
Her story has become my story:
she planted a seed inside me
before I was born.
Now life has freed her,
let her tendrils blossom,
uncurl to the tips of my fingers,
the dead ends of hair,
where she resides in splendour,
luminous as a carcinoma
beyond the biologist's lens.

Beyond the biologist's lens,
luminous as a carcinoma
where she resides in splendour,
the dead ends of hair
uncurl to the tips of my fingers,
let her tendrils blossom
now life has freed her.
Before I was born
she planted a seed inside me:
her story has become my story.
In the pit of my belly
sometimes she curls around her pain,
always close.
In an infant sling, she weighs me down –
I carry my mother on my back.

Tokyo Station

(Inspired by the black-and-white city photos of Daido Moriyama)

This is the way a man looks
just in front of the safety line
before he jumps.
It is the same as the face of a man
waiting for a train
but more focused.
Those other faces, those
are the faces of people
waiting for a train.
They stand with shoulders slumped,
arms folded, one foot forward,
eyes towards the tunnel, hoping.
He alone looks straight across,
expressionless, at the other platform;
body straight, shoulders back,
best clothes on –
waiting for the smell like burnt rubber,
the vibration of the track.

Gracefully

Once my young hand skimmed
the inside of an old man's arm
accidentally. It was as soft
as my first friend's newborn child:
skin that had not known weather.

Surprising as a web's fine touch
on faces, age is not as we expect.
White and grey are colours of a dove,
each with its own beauty.

You hide your photos, shocked
by visions of a waist no longer slim.
I have known youth: its taut form
draws no desire.

These days I stroke the inside of my arm
and touch silk.

For My Lost Child

I asked for your name to be put
on a little boat,
and the boat should not be blue or pink -
not even yellow –
but white, like the tiny cardigans
my mother used to knit,
then smoothed with long fingers
now gone where you are.
Then suddenly, at the thought of you
as a little boat,
alone, empty, unused,
while people party in a larger boat
or flirt on shore,
I cried
and watched a while as you rose
and fell, gently, pulling at your rope
that will not come untied
or ever let you go.

APRILIA ZANK

Dr. Aprilia Zank is a freelance lecturer for Creative Writing and Translation in the Department of Languages and Communication at the Ludwig Maximilian University of Munich, Germany. She was born in Romania, and in her twenties she moved to Germany where she received her PhD degree in Literature and Psycholinguistics from the Ludwig Maximilian University for her thesis *THE WORD IN THE WORD Literary Text Reception and Linguistic Relativity.*

Aprilia is also a poet and a translator, and the editor of the English–German anthology *poetry tREnD Eine englisch-deutsche Anthologie zeitgenössischer Lyrik.* She writes verse in English and German, and was awarded a distinction at the "Vera Piller" Poetry Contest in Zurich. Her poetry collection *TERMINUS ARCADIA* was 2nd Place Winner at the Twowolvz Press Poetry Chapbook Contest 2013. She translates from and into English, German, French and Romanian in collaborative projects with various artists.

Aprilia is also a passionate photographer.

Beyond borders of any kind and barriers of language, faith or Weltanschauung, poetry connects people all over the world, as carrier of universal yearnings, visions, emotions, fears... translated into the language of metaphors. The new media make poetic encounters and cultural exchange possible, irrespective of distance and time, and artists who can so easily connect in the virtual world are often motivated to meet in person, too.

Leda and the Swan

not the white of snow
or the velvet feathers
drove you to surrender
but the strength of muscle
against reluctant fibres
the taste of blood
on your thighs
ancestral instincts
gushing
in the rhythm of motion
opening the eyes
of your mind
wide
at the radiance of light
sensed in your lap
the numinous stir
tensing your breast
under the numb weight
of feathers
the otherness
of the embrace
the grasp of the beak
on your neck
the mystery of
wings and arms
growing together

(published in *morphrog #6,* Jan. 2013, The Frogmore Press)

Wednesdays

Wednesdays in this bar
close to the hospital
where they came
for the monthly check
sitting
almost at the same table
I was shuddering at the thought
that their skin
might touch my skin

while trying some conversation
I was thinking
of this lake
with the host of water lilies
such a waste of beauty
for hardly anyone to see
the banks so slippery
mud and weeds
clinging to your feet

back to my flat
had to find my way
blindly
bumped into walls
bruised my knuckles
because of the burnt out bulbs
in the stairway.

(published in *EgoPHobia* #34, May 2012)

poppies

the flash of poppies
on waxen skin
blades triumph
in clean-cut
callous
parallels

owl calls
on bare branches
fluorescent rags
lit by fake moons
mildew silences lust
cells darken in stop-baths
synaptic countdowns
flicker
on thinning silver

yellow teeth grin
devour to soothe
cuddle
infant awe
in a muddle of syllables

tissue starves
for the flash of poppies

walls

black and moss-green walls
witnesses of
chivalrous virtues
cast-iron chastity
perennial stones
echoes
of transient crossing
of lifelines
the heat of the breath
freezes into atonal accords
kisses hang
on ghostly tree branches
like molested birds
under a conspicuous moon

(published in *Musings: A Mosaic,* Poets Corner Anthology, 2012)

preparing for the death on stage (II)

the bride wore black and a scar
and she was another man's bride
the wedding guests
having come uninvited
scuttled away their small rounds
scattered last year's spare seeds
left
short of applause

from beneath the ice
the Infant stares
at heavenless skies
while little fish
nibble
at the blue of his irises

they had treasured the guilt
in leaden cases
in redoubts of memory
but the deeds of hands
corroded
leaked
crept
settled like oil
on the broth of the day

enter the Judge
with his white cane
fumbles for paragraphs
while the defendants
wearing identical uniforms
prepare for the last bow

(published in *morphrog* #7, July 2013, The Frogmore Press)

when they came

when they came
to open my chest
I asked them
according to which
paragraphs
I had not sent them
to the scaffold
not even known them
when the blood burst
I was in the desert
washing the dust
off my tiny feet
in a tin can
in the seclusion
of my forefathers' prayers
caressing the lambs
before slaughter
straining my senses
to hear the flute
and perceive
my golden shoes

I asked them
when they came
but there was no answer
only the clink
of scalpels
and the silver chime
of opening lilies

(published in *morphrog* #6, Jan. 2013, The Frogmore Press)